Chapter 1: Introduction

A few years ago, I attended a networking event where I felt completely out of place. I watched as people around me effortlessly engaged in conversations, exchanged business cards, and formed connections. Meanwhile, I stood awkwardly on the sidelines, unsure of how to start a conversation. I realized that despite my professional success, I lacked a crucial skill: the ability to talk to anyone with confidence.

Communication is the backbone of every relationship, whether personal or professional. Yet, many of us struggle with it. We find ourselves at a loss for words during important meetings, social gatherings, or even casual encounters. This inability can lead to missed opportunities, strained relationships, and a lack of personal growth.

But what if I told you that you could change this? What if there was a way to develop the skills needed to engage in meaningful conversations with anyone, anywhere? This book, "How to Talk to Anyone: Success Skills to Talk with Anyone in Business and Personal Environments," offers just that. It provides you with the tools and techniques to navigate any social or professional setting with ease.

Imagine walking into a room and feeling an instant connection with the people around you. Picture yourself leading discussions, making lasting impressions, and building strong relationships. These are the benefits you can expect when you master the art of conversation. You'll not only improve your social interactions but also boost your confidence, enhance your career prospects, and enrich your personal life.

I am Debra Miller, and I have spent 40 years working in real estate, banking, and finance. Throughout my career, I have seen firsthand the impact that effective communication can have on success. I have also experienced the frustration of not knowing how to connect with others. This book is a result of my journey to overcome that challenge. It combines practical advice with real-life examples to guide you in developing the skills you need to talk to anyone.

Here's what you can expect from this book. Each chapter focuses on a specific aspect of communication, from starting a conversation to listening actively and asking the right questions. You will learn how to read body language, use humor, and handle difficult discussions. The book also addresses common hurdles, such as overcoming shyness and dealing with rejection.

To keep you engaged, the book includes exercises and tips that you can apply in your daily life. These practical tools will help you build your confidence and improve your communication skills over time. By the end of this journey, you will feel more comfortable and capable in any social or professional setting.

I encourage you to take an active role in your learning. Practice the techniques outlined in this book, reflect on your experiences, and seek feedback from others. Remember, communication is a skill that can be developed with practice and persistence.

So, let's embark on this journey together. Let's explore the strategies and insights that will empower you to talk to anyone with confidence. Whether you're looking to advance in your career, build stronger personal relationships, or simply feel more at ease in social settings, this book is your guide. The tools and techniques you will learn here are not just theoretical; they are practical and proven methods that I have used and seen work for others.

In conclusion, effective communication is not just a skill; it's a key to unlocking opportunities and building meaningful connections. By the end of this book, you will have the confidence and ability to engage in successful conversations in any environment. So, dive in, practice the techniques, and watch as your ability to connect with others transforms your personal and professional life. The journey to becoming a great conversationalist starts here. Are you ready?

Chapter 2: Building Confidence in Social Settings

Think back to the last time you walked into a room full of strangers. Perhaps it was a networking event, a party, or even a new workplace. Did you feel an immediate sense of ease, or did a wave of anxiety wash over you, making you second-guess every move and word? For many, the latter is all too familiar. This chapter is dedicated to transforming that anxiety into confidence, turning every social interaction into an opportunity for connection and growth.

2.1 Mastering the First Impression

Making a strong first impression is crucial. Research shows that people form lasting opinions within the first seven seconds of meeting someone. This phenomenon, known as the "7-second rule," means that those initial moments can set the tone for the rest of your interaction. The psychological basis for this, called the primacy effect, suggests that information presented first has a more significant impact on perception than information introduced later. This is why your first impression is often the most memorable and influential.

Your appearance and grooming play a pivotal role in how you are perceived. Dressing appropriately for different contexts is not just about fashion; it's about respect and understanding the social norms of each setting. Whether it's a business meeting, a casual brunch, or a formal event, your attire should align with the occasion. Personal hygiene is equally important. Cleanliness, neat hair, and well-maintained nails can significantly boost your confidence and the way others perceive you. A polished appearance demonstrates that you care about yourself and respect those around you.

Body language and posture are silent yet powerful communicators. Standing tall with shoulders back not only conveys confidence but also makes you feel more self-assured. Open gestures, such as keeping your hands visible and avoiding crossed arms, make you appear approachable and friendly. These non-verbal cues can significantly impact how others perceive you, often before you even say a word. Practicing good posture and open body language can help you project confidence and invite positive interactions.

Verbal introduction techniques are essential for making a memorable first impression. Crafting a compelling elevator pitch can be a game-changer. Your pitch should succinctly convey who you are, what you do, and why it matters, all within a few sentences. This clarity and conciseness can leave a lasting impression on your listener. Additionally, a firm handshake paired with direct eye contact can further reinforce your confidence. These elements, when combined, create a powerful introduction that sets the stage for a meaningful conversation.

Mastering the first impression involves a combination of appearance, body language, and verbal communication. Understanding the psychological underpinnings, such as the primacy effect, can help you appreciate the importance of these initial moments. By paying attention to your grooming, adopting confident body language, and perfecting your verbal introductions, you can ensure that your first impression is both positive and lasting.

Remember, the goal is to present the best version of yourself in those crucial first moments. This doesn't mean you have to be perfect or put on a facade. Authenticity is key. People are drawn to genuine individuals who are comfortable in their own skin. By focusing on these aspects, you can approach any social setting with confidence, knowing that you have the tools to make a strong and positive first impression. As you practice and refine these skills, they will become second nature, allowing you to navigate social interactions with ease and confidence.

2.2 Overcoming Social Anxiety with Mindfulness

Social anxiety can be a crippling barrier, preventing meaningful interactions and stifling personal growth. It manifests in various ways: racing thoughts, sweating, trembling, and an overwhelming urge to avoid social settings. The heart races, palms get clammy, and the mind becomes a whirlpool of negative thoughts. Common triggers include speaking in public, meeting new people, or even engaging in casual conversations. For some, the mere thought of entering a room full of strangers can induce panic. This anxiety doesn't just affect personal life; it spills over into professional settings, hampering career growth and opportunities.

Mindfulness offers a powerful tool to manage this anxiety. It involves paying attention to the present moment without judgment, helping you observe your reactions and understand their origins. Breathing exercises are a cornerstone of mindfulness and can be incredibly effective in calming nerves. A simple exercise involves taking slow, deep breaths, focusing on the sensation of air entering and leaving the body. This practice can slow the heart rate and create a sense of calm. Grounding exercises, such as feeling the texture of an object or focusing on the sensation of your feet on the ground, can help you stay present and reduce anxiety.

Cognitive Behavioral Therapy (CBT) provides another layer of support, helping to reframe anxious thoughts. This approach involves identifying and challenging negative self-talk, which often fuels social anxiety. For example, if you catch yourself thinking, "I'll make a fool of myself," CBT encourages you to counter this with a more positive and realistic thought, like "I've prepared well, and I can handle this situation." Creating realistic and positive affirmations can also be beneficial. Statements like "I am capable and prepared" or "I can connect with others" can reinforce a positive mindset and reduce anxiety.

Practical Exercises

Daily mindfulness meditation can significantly impact your ability to manage social anxiety. Set aside a few minutes each day to practice mindful breathing or body scan exercises. These practices help you become more aware of your thoughts and feelings without becoming overwhelmed by them. Visualization techniques can also be valuable. Before entering a social situation, take a moment to visualize a positive outcome. Imagine yourself engaging confidently in conversation, receiving positive responses, and feeling relaxed. This mental rehearsal can prepare you for actual interactions and reduce anxiety.

By integrating mindfulness techniques and CBT strategies, you can develop a toolkit to navigate social anxiety effectively. These practices not only help manage anxiety in the moment but also build long-term resilience, allowing you to approach social situations with greater confidence and ease.

2.3 Strategies for Starting Conversations with Strangers

Starting a conversation with a stranger can be daunting, but choosing the right context can make all the difference. Networking events and social gatherings are fertile grounds for initiating discussions. These settings are inherently designed for mingling, making it easier to approach someone. For instance, at a networking event, people expect to be approached and are often more open to conversation. Similarly, social gatherings like parties or community events offer a relaxed atmosphere where informal chats are welcomed. In these environments, everyone is typically there to connect, share experiences, and enjoy the event, providing a natural segue into conversation.

Casual settings like cafes or public transportation can also present opportunities. Imagine sitting in a cozy coffee shop, the aroma of freshly brewed coffee wafting through the air, and spotting someone engrossed in a book you recently read. This shared interest provides a perfect icebreaker. Public transportation, while a bit trickier due to the transient nature of the interaction, can still offer moments for brief, meaningful exchanges. A simple comment on the day's weather or a question about a shared destination can break the ice without feeling intrusive.

Effective icebreakers are crucial for setting a positive tone. Commenting on the environment or event is a reliable way to start. For example, at a conference, you might say, "The keynote speaker was really inspiring, don't you think?" This type of comment is neutral, inviting the other person to share their thoughts. Asking open-ended questions is another powerful technique. Questions like "What brought you to this event?" or "How do you know the host?" encourage the other person to open up, providing a natural flow to the conversation.

These questions show genuine interest and can lead to deeper discussions.

Active listening is fundamental to building rapport. When someone speaks, they want to feel heard and understood. Nodding and using verbal affirmations like "I see" or "That's interesting" can show that you are engaged. Reflective listening, which involves paraphrasing the speaker's words, can further demonstrate your attentiveness. For instance, if someone says, "I've been working on a challenging project at work," you might respond, "It sounds like your project has been quite demanding." This technique not only shows you are listening but also encourages the speaker to continue sharing.

Handling rejection is a part of initiating conversations. Not every attempt will result in a meaningful exchange, and that's okay. Normalizing rejection as part of the process can help mitigate its sting. Understand that if someone is not interested in talking, it is not a reflection of your worth. They might be preoccupied or simply not in the mood to chat. Moving on without taking it personally is crucial. A polite smile and a simple, "It was nice meeting you," can gracefully end the interaction and leave the door open for future conversations.

In summary, starting conversations with strangers becomes easier when you understand the context, use effective icebreakers, practice active listening, and handle rejection with grace. Whether you're at a bustling networking event or a quiet cafe, these strategies can help you navigate social interactions with confidence and ease.

2.4 Using Positive Self-Talk to Boost Confidence

Your internal dialogue, the continuous stream of thoughts running through your mind, plays a significant role in shaping your self-perception and confidence. Research indicates that positive self-talk can elevate your mood and enhance your belief in your abilities. Conversely, negative self-talk can reinforce feelings of inadequacy and self-doubt. For instance, telling yourself, "I always mess up in social situations," can create a self-fulfilling prophecy, increasing anxiety and making you more likely to falter. On the other hand, reminding yourself, "I am capable and prepared," can help you approach interactions with a confident mindset.

The science behind self-talk and confidence is compelling. Studies have shown that positive self-talk can improve performance by boosting self-efficacy—the belief in your ability to succeed in specific situations. This concept, rooted in cognitive psychology, suggests that our thoughts influence our emotions and behaviors. When you engage in positive self-talk, you are essentially rewiring your brain to create a more optimistic outlook, which can significantly impact your interactions and overall confidence.

To cultivate a positive internal dialogue, start by replacing negative thoughts with positive affirmations. When you catch yourself thinking, "I'm terrible at this," counter it with, "I am learning and improving every day." This simple shift can make a profound difference in how you perceive yourself and your abilities. Daily journaling can also reinforce positive beliefs. Spend a few minutes each day writing down your accomplishments, no matter how small. This practice helps you focus on your strengths and achievements, creating a positive feedback loop that boosts your confidence over time.

Mantras and affirmations are powerful tools for enhancing self-talk. Crafting personalized affirmations that resonate with you can be particularly effective. For example, if you struggle with public speaking, an affirmation like, "I communicate my ideas clearly and confidently," can be a valuable addition to your daily routine. Integrate these affirmations into your day by repeating them during quiet moments, such as while brushing your teeth or commuting to work. Over time, these positive statements can become ingrained in your subconscious, subtly shifting your self-perception.

Breaking free from negative thought patterns requires more than just positive affirmations. Cognitive restructuring exercises can help you challenge and change these harmful thought cycles. Start by identifying a negative thought and examining the evidence supporting and contradicting it. For instance, if you think, "No one wants to talk to me," list instances where people have shown interest in your company. This exercise helps you see the irrationality of your negative thoughts and encourages a more balanced perspective.

Practicing gratitude is another effective strategy for self-affirmation. By focusing on the positive aspects of your life, you can shift your mindset from one of scarcity to one of abundance. Each day, write down three things you are grateful for. These can be as simple as a delicious meal or a supportive friend. Over time, this practice can help you develop a more positive outlook, which naturally enhances your confidence.

Integrating these techniques into your daily routine can significantly boost your confidence and transform your interactions. Positive self-talk, affirmations, cognitive restructuring, and gratitude practices are not quick fixes;

they require consistent effort and practice. However, the rewards are well worth it. As you cultivate a more positive internal dialogue, you will find yourself approaching social and professional situations with greater ease and confidence. This shift in mindset can open doors to new opportunities and enrich your personal and professional relationships.

2.5 Practicing Assertiveness in Everyday Situations

Understanding assertiveness is crucial for anyone looking to improve their communication skills. Assertiveness means expressing your thoughts, feelings, and needs in a direct, honest, and respectful way. It stands in stark contrast to passivity, where one might avoid expressing their needs or opinions to avoid conflict, often leading to feelings of resentment and frustration. On the other hand, aggression involves expressing one's needs in a forceful and disrespectful manner, which can lead to conflicts and damaged relationships. By practicing assertive communication, you find a healthy balance that respects both your own needs and the needs of others.

The benefits of assertive communication are numerous. It helps reduce stress, as you no longer feel burdened by the weight of unexpressed feelings or unmet needs. It also fosters stronger relationships by building mutual respect and understanding. When you communicate assertively, you are more likely to achieve your goals and gain the respect of others. This type of communication can also enhance your self-esteem, as you become more confident in expressing yourself and standing up for your rights.

A key technique in assertive communication is the use of "I" statements. These statements allow you to express your feelings and needs without blaming or criticizing others. For example, instead of saying, "You never listen to me," you might say, "I feel unheard when you talk over me." This approach focuses on your experience rather than accusing the other person, making it more likely that they will respond positively. "I" statements help to open up a dialogue, encouraging the other person to understand your perspective and work towards a resolution.

Setting and respecting personal boundaries is another essential aspect of assertiveness. Boundaries define what you are comfortable with and how you expect others to treat you. Clear boundaries help prevent misunderstandings and protect your well-being. For instance, if you need uninterrupted time to focus on a project, you might say, "I need to work without interruptions for the next hour; can we discuss this later?" This statement clearly communicates your need while showing respect for the other person's concerns.

Role-playing scenarios are invaluable for practicing assertiveness. Try practicing with a friend or in front of a mirror. For example, rehearse a situation where you need to say "no" to additional work that you cannot handle. Practice maintaining eye contact, using a calm tone, and standing firm in your decision. Handling pushback is also crucial. If someone reacts negatively to your assertiveness, stay composed and reiterate your needs calmly. For example, if a colleague insists on adding more to your workload, you might respond, "I understand this is important, but I cannot take on more tasks right now without compromising the quality of my work."

In real-life applications, assertiveness can be transformative. Consider asking for a raise at work. This can be intimidating, but by using assertive communication, you can present your case confidently.

Start by preparing your points: your achievements, contributions to the team, and reasons why you deserve a raise. During the conversation, use "I" statements to express your needs, such as, "I believe my contributions have significantly impacted our team's success, and I would like to discuss a potential raise." This approach shows that you value yourself and your work while inviting a constructive discussion.

Resolving conflicts in personal relationships is another area where assertiveness is vital. Imagine a situation where a friend frequently cancels plans at the last minute. Instead of harboring resentment, address the issue directly. You might say, "I feel disappointed when our plans get canceled last minute because I look forward to our time together. Can we find a way to plan that works better for both of us?" This statement expresses your feelings without blaming your friend, opening the door for a solution that respects both parties' needs.

By practicing assertiveness in these everyday situations, you can build stronger, more respectful relationships and enhance your confidence. Assertive communication is a skill that can be developed with practice, and its benefits extend across all areas of your life.

2.6 The Power of Small Wins: Celebrating Social Successes

Understanding the concept of small wins can revolutionize the way you approach building confidence. Small wins are minor achievements that, when accumulated, create a significant positive impact on your overall self-esteem and motivation. Psychologically, acknowledging these small successes can trigger a release of dopamine, the brain's "feel-good" neurotransmitter. This release not only boosts your mood but also reinforces the behavior, making you more likely to repeat it. Over time, these small wins build momentum, creating a cascade of positive reinforcement that bolsters your confidence and encourages you to take on larger challenges.

Tracking your progress is crucial in recognizing and celebrating these small wins. One effective method is to maintain a social interactions journal. In this journal, note down each successful interaction, no matter how minor it may seem. Did you initiate a conversation with a colleague? Write it down. Did you make a new acquaintance at a networking event? Record it. This practice not only helps you keep track of your progress but also allows you to reflect on your growth over time. Additionally, setting and achieving small, incremental goals can provide a sense of accomplishment and keep you motivated. These goals might include speaking up in a meeting, attending a social event, or practicing a new communication technique.

Celebrating your achievements, no matter how small, is essential for reinforcing positive behavior. Rewarding yourself for meeting social goals can be as simple as treating yourself to your favorite coffee or taking a relaxing bath. These rewards create an association between effort and pleasure, making you more inclined to continue pushing yourself. Sharing your successes with supportive friends or family can also enhance the celebratory experience. When you share your achievements, you not only receive external validation but also inspire those around you, creating a positive feedback loop.

Maintaining motivation is a continuous process that requires intentional effort. Creating a vision board for your social goals can serve as a constant visual reminder of what you are working towards. Fill it with images and words that represent your aspirations, whether it's becoming a more confident speaker, building a robust professional network, or simply feeling more comfortable in social settings. This visual representation can keep you focused and inspired. Joining support groups or finding an accountability partner can also provide the encouragement and motivation needed to stay on track. Having someone to share your journey with can make the process more enjoyable and provide a sense of camaraderie.

Interactive Exercise: Creating Your Vision Board

Materials Needed:

- A board or large piece of paper
- Magazines, printouts, or images
- Scissors, glue, markers

Steps:

1. Reflect on your social goals and aspirations.
2. Gather images and words that represent these goals.
3. Arrange and glue them onto your board.
4. Place the vision board somewhere you will see it daily.

In summary, the power of small wins lies in their cumulative effect on building confidence and fostering continuous improvement. By tracking progress, celebrating achievements, and maintaining motivation, you create a sustainable path toward becoming a more confident and effective communicator. These incremental steps not only enhance your social interactions but also contribute to your overall personal and professional growth. Embrace the small wins, and watch as they transform your ability to connect with others, one step at a time.

Chapter 3: Mastering Nonverbal Communication

Picture yourself at a crowded conference, scanning the room for familiar faces. Amid the sea of attendees, your eyes meet someone who mirrors your nervous smile. Instantly, you feel a connection, a silent understanding. This interaction, devoid of words, underscores the profound power of nonverbal communication. Our gestures, postures, and expressions convey emotions and intentions more eloquently than words often can. This chapter explores how to interpret and use these nonverbal cues to enhance your social interactions.

3.1 Interpreting Common Gestures and Postures

Understanding the nuances of body language is akin to learning a new language. Each gesture and posture carries its own meaning, often revealing more than the words we speak. One of the most frequently encountered gestures is crossing arms. This simple act can indicate a defensive or closed-off stance. When someone crosses their arms, they might be feeling guarded, uncomfortable, or resistant to what's being said. However, context is key. If the room is cold, crossed arms might just signify a need for warmth.

Another common gesture is placing hands on hips. This posture often conveys assertiveness or impatience. When someone stands with their hands on their hips, they might be asserting their authority or signaling that they are ready for action. However, this gesture can also be a sign of frustration or impatience, especially if accompanied by other cues like a furrowed brow or tapping foot. Understanding these subtle variations can help you gauge the emotional state of the person you're interacting with.

Contextual interpretation plays a crucial role in decoding body language. Take nodding, for example. In most situations, nodding signifies agreement or encourages the speaker to continue. However, a slow, deliberate nod can indicate skepticism or a need for further clarification. Similarly, scratching one's head typically signifies confusion or uncertainty. But in some contexts, like during a presentation, it might simply be a sign of deep thought or concentration. Being aware of the surrounding circumstances can help you accurately interpret these gestures.

Cultural variations add another layer of complexity to nonverbal communication. The thumbs-up gesture, for instance, is viewed positively in many Western cultures, signifying approval or agreement. However, in some parts of Greece and the Middle East, this same gesture can be considered offensive. Eye contact is another area where cultural norms differ significantly. In Western cultures, making direct eye contact is seen as a sign of confidence and respect. Yet, in many Asian cultures, prolonged eye contact can be perceived as rude or confrontational. Understanding these cultural differences is vital, especially in a globalized world where cross-cultural interactions are commonplace.

Practical applications of gesture interpretation are numerous and can significantly enhance your social and professional interactions. During a job interview, for example, decoding the interviewer's body language can provide valuable insights. If the interviewer leans forward and maintains eye contact, it often signifies interest and engagement. Conversely, if they frequently glance at their watch or cross their arms, it might indicate impatience or disinterest. Similarly, understanding audience reactions during a presentation can help you adjust your delivery in real-time. Noticing nods and smiles can encourage you to continue, while confused expressions or lack of eye contact might signal a need to clarify your points further.

Interactive Exercise: Body Language Observation

Spend a day observing the body language of people around you in various settings such as work, social gatherings, or public places. Note down specific gestures and postures and try to interpret their meanings based on the context. Reflect on how these observations enhance your understanding of nonverbal communication.

In sum, mastering the interpretation of common gestures and postures requires an awareness of both context and cultural variations. By honing these skills, you can unlock a deeper level of understanding in your interactions, allowing you to communicate more effectively and build stronger connections with those around you.

3.2 The Art of Mirroring for Building Rapport

Mirroring is a fascinating and powerful way to build rapport with others. At its core, mirroring involves unconsciously imitating another person's body language, speech patterns, and even facial expressions. This behavior is deeply rooted in our evolutionary past, where mimicking others helped early humans build trust and social bonds crucial for survival. Mirroring often happens naturally and is a subtle form of communication that signals empathy and understanding. This unconscious mimicry, known as the chameleon effect, can make interactions smoother and more harmonious. When you mirror someone, you reflect their emotions and behaviors, making them feel understood and connected to you.

To use mirroring effectively, start by observing the other person's posture and gestures. If they lean forward, you might do the same. If they cross their legs, you could mirror this gesture subtly. The goal is to match their body language without being obvious. This creates a sense of similarity and connection. Another key aspect is reflecting the other person's emotional state. If they are excited and animated, respond with similar enthusiasm. If they are calm and reserved, adopt a more subdued demeanor. By aligning your behavior with theirs, you foster a sense of mutual understanding and comfort.

Timing and pacing are crucial elements in successful mirroring. It's important to wait a few moments before mimicking the other person's actions to avoid appearing insincere or robotic. Gradually increasing the level of mirroring can make the interaction feel more natural. For instance, if someone gestures with their hands while speaking, you might start by lightly nodding in agreement before eventually incorporating similar hand movements. This gradual approach ensures that your mirroring feels authentic and helps build a genuine connection.

Mirroring can be particularly effective in various contexts. In a sales meeting, for example, building rapport with a potential client is essential. By subtly mirroring their body language and speech patterns, you can create a sense of trust and familiarity. If the client leans in to discuss a point, you can do the same, showing that you are engaged and interested. This technique can help you establish a positive relationship, making the client more likely to be receptive to your pitch.

On a first date, mirroring can help enhance the connection and make the interaction more comfortable. If your date is animated and expressive, responding with similar energy can create a sense of harmony and excitement. Conversely, if they are more reserved and thoughtful, adopting a calm and reflective demeanor can help build a deeper bond. By tuning into their emotional state and reflecting it, you show that you are genuinely interested and attuned to their feelings.

In professional settings, mirroring can also be a valuable tool for effective communication. During a team meeting, for instance, mirroring the body language of your colleagues can create a sense of unity and collaboration. If a team member is enthusiastic about a project, responding with similar enthusiasm can reinforce their ideas and encourage a positive team dynamic. This approach fosters a supportive environment where everyone feels valued and understood.

Mirroring is not just about copying behaviors; it's about creating a sense of connection and understanding. By paying attention to the other person's body language, speech patterns, and emotional state, you can build rapport and foster positive interactions. This technique, when used thoughtfully and subtly, can enhance your communication skills and help you connect with others on a deeper level. Whether you're in a business meeting, on a first date, or interacting with colleagues, mirroring can make your interactions more meaningful and successful.

3.3 Using Facial Expressions to Convey Emotions

Facial expressions serve as a window into our emotions, often conveying what words cannot. They play a pivotal role in nonverbal communication, helping us express feelings like happiness, sadness, anger, and surprise. These basic emotions are universal; regardless of cultural background, a smile signals joy, while a frown indicates displeasure. The ability to read and interpret these expressions can significantly enhance your interactions, making you more empathetic and responsive to others' feelings.

Reading facial cues involves paying attention to both macro-expressions and micro-expressions. Macro-expressions are the obvious facial movements we make, like a broad smile or a deep scowl. These are easy to spot and interpret. However, micro-expressions are brief, involuntary facial expressions that flash across a person's face for just a fraction of a second. They often reveal true emotions that someone might be trying to hide. For example, a quick flash of anger or sadness might appear before the person's face returns to a neutral state. Becoming adept at recognizing these fleeting expressions can provide deeper insights into what someone is truly feeling.

Eye movements offer another layer of understanding. When someone looks up and to the right, they might be recalling a memory, whereas looking up and to the left could indicate they're constructing a thought or imagining a scenario. Rapid blinking can signal anxiety or stress, while dilated pupils might indicate interest or attraction. These subtle cues, when combined with other facial expressions, can give you a comprehensive understanding of the person's emotional state.

Aligning your facial expressions with your spoken words is crucial for conveying sincerity. A genuine smile, for instance, involves not just the mouth but also the eyes, creating what is known as a Duchenne smile. This type of smile signals genuine warmth and friendliness. In contrast, a forced smile that doesn't reach the eyes can come across as insincere. Similarly, maintaining a neutral expression while listening shows attentiveness and respect, indicating that you are fully engaged in the conversation. This alignment between verbal and nonverbal cues creates a cohesive and trustworthy interaction.

To practice interpreting and using facial expressions, start by observing and mimicking expressions in a mirror. This exercise helps you become more aware of your facial muscles and how they move. Try expressing different emotions like happiness, sadness, anger, and surprise, and observe how your face changes. Another useful exercise is watching TV shows with the sound off. Focus on the actors' faces and try to interpret their emotions and thoughts based solely on their expressions. This practice sharpens your ability to read facial cues without relying on verbal context.

Understanding the role of facial expressions in communication can transform the way you connect with others. Whether you're in a business meeting, a social gathering, or a casual conversation, accurately interpreting and aligning your facial expressions with your words can make your interactions more genuine and impactful. This skill not only enhances your ability to communicate but also builds stronger, more empathetic relationships.

3.4 Perfecting Eye Contact for Connection

Eye contact is a powerful tool in nonverbal communication, crucial for building trust and connection. When you make eye contact, you signal attention and interest, showing the other person that you are engaged and present in the conversation. It creates a sense of mutual respect and understanding, making the interaction more meaningful. Beyond signaling interest, eye contact can also establish dominance or submission, depending on the context. In professional settings, maintaining steady eye contact can convey confidence and authority, while looking away too often may suggest uncertainty or lack of confidence.

To effectively use eye contact, consider the 70/30 rule, which suggests maintaining eye contact for about 70% of the time while listening and 30% while speaking. This balance helps create a comfortable yet attentive atmosphere. Another technique is the "triangle" method, where you shift your gaze between the other person's eyes and mouth. This subtle movement keeps your gaze natural and prevents it from becoming too intense. Practicing these techniques can help you master eye contact, making your interactions more engaging and authentic.

Avoiding common mistakes is essential for effective eye contact. One pitfall is staring, which can make the other person uncomfortable and create a sense of intrusion. Instead, aim for a steady gaze that conveys interest without being overpowering. On the flip side, shifty eyes can signal dishonesty or nervousness. Practicing a steady gaze can help you avoid this. You can improve by practicing in front of a mirror or during video calls, gradually building your comfort level. These small adjustments can significantly impact how you are perceived in both personal and professional interactions.

Cultural sensitivity is another crucial aspect of eye contact. In Western cultures, direct eye contact is often expected and seen as a sign of confidence and respect. However, in some Asian cultures, prolonged eye contact can be considered disrespectful or confrontational. Understanding these cultural differences can help you navigate interactions more effectively. Adjusting your eye contact based on the cultural context ensures that you communicate respect and avoid misunderstandings. For instance, if you are interacting with someone from a culture where direct eye contact is less common, a softer gaze or shorter eye contact duration might be more appropriate.

In a business meeting, maintaining eye contact can help you assert your ideas and show that you are confident and knowledgeable. Meanwhile, during a casual conversation with friends or family, eye contact can deepen the connection and show that you value their presence. In sales, eye contact can be a powerful tool to build trust with potential clients. By demonstrating that you are fully engaged, you can create a sense of reliability and professionalism, making the client more likely to trust and engage with you.

Mastering eye contact involves a delicate balance of maintaining interest without making the other person uncomfortable. It requires practice and awareness of both cultural norms and individual comfort levels. By incorporating these techniques and understanding the nuances of eye contact, you can enhance your communication skills, building stronger, more meaningful connections in various aspects of your life. Whether you are presenting in a high-stakes meeting, networking at an event, or simply having a heartfelt conversation with a friend, effective eye contact can make all the difference.

3.5 Understanding Personal Space and Proxemics

Imagine you're at a bustling networking event, weaving through the crowd as you look for familiar faces. Suddenly, you find yourself in a conversation with someone who steps a bit too close, making you feel uneasy. This discomfort is a subtle yet powerful aspect of personal space, known as proxemics. Proxemics is the study of how humans use space in communication, and it's crucial for understanding social interactions. Personal space can be divided into four zones: intimate, personal, social, and public. Intimate space is reserved for close friends and family, typically within 18 inches. Personal space extends from 18 inches to 4 feet and is for interactions with friends and acquaintances. Social space, ranging from 4 to 12 feet, is used for interactions in social or professional settings. Beyond 12 feet is public space, suitable for public speaking or addressing large groups. The distance we maintain can significantly affect the dynamics of our interactions, influencing comfort levels and the nature of the conversation.

Cultural variations play a significant role in personal space preferences, adding another layer of complexity. In Mediterranean cultures, close proximity is common and often signifies warmth and friendliness. People from these regions may stand closer during conversations, touch more frequently, and feel comfortable with less personal space. In contrast, Northern European cultures typically maintain greater personal distance. People from these areas may prefer to keep others at arm's length, viewing close proximity as intrusive. Understanding these cultural differences can help you navigate social interactions more effectively, especially in diverse environments. Recognizing and respecting these preferences can prevent misunderstandings and foster positive relationships.

Recognizing and respecting others' space boundaries is key to comfortable interactions. Signs of discomfort when personal space is invaded include stepping back, turning away, or crossing arms. These cues indicate that the person needs more space. Adjusting your proximity based on context and reactions can enhance your interactions. For example, in a professional meeting, maintaining a social distance of about 4 to 12 feet is appropriate, signaling respect and professionalism. In a more personal setting, like a gathering with friends, a closer distance within the personal space zone is acceptable and can help build rapport. Being mindful of these subtle cues and adjusting accordingly can make your interactions smoother and more comfortable for everyone involved.

Practical applications of managing personal space are numerous and can greatly enhance your social and professional interactions. At a crowded networking event, navigating personal space can be challenging. In such settings, aim to maintain a comfortable social distance, even in tight spaces. If you notice someone stepping back or looking uneasy, it's a sign to give them more room. In professional meetings, maintaining appropriate distance is crucial. Sitting or standing too close to colleagues or clients can make them uncomfortable and affect the outcome of the interaction. Ensure you position yourself at a respectful distance, typically within the social space zone, to foster a professional atmosphere. Being aware of these dynamics can help you create positive and productive interactions in various settings.

In a business context, understanding and respecting personal space is vital for building strong relationships and fostering a positive working environment. For instance, during a one-on-one meeting with a client, maintaining a social distance can help create a sense of professionalism and respect. This distance allows for comfortable conversation while respecting the client's need for personal space. Similarly, in team meetings, arranging seating to allow for adequate personal space can enhance comfort and encourage open communication. By being mindful of personal space, you can create an environment where everyone feels respected and valued, leading to more effective and harmonious interactions.

In social settings, managing personal space is equally important for building and maintaining relationships. At a party or social gathering, being aware of personal space can help you navigate interactions more smoothly. If you notice someone stepping back or appearing uncomfortable, it's a cue to give them more space. Conversely, if someone leans in and engages closely, it indicates they are comfortable with a closer distance. Adjusting your proximity based on these cues can help you build rapport and make others feel at ease. Understanding and respecting personal space in social interactions can enhance your ability to connect with others and build meaningful relationships.

By understanding proxemics and being mindful of personal space, you can navigate social and professional interactions more effectively. Recognizing cultural variations and adjusting your behavior based on context and reactions can enhance your communication skills and foster positive relationships. Whether you're at a networking event, a professional meeting, or a social gathering, being aware of personal space can make your interactions more comfortable and successful. This awareness and adaptability can help you build stronger connections and navigate diverse social landscapes with ease.

3.6 The Role of Touch in Social Interactions

Touch is a powerful form of nonverbal communication that can profoundly influence social interactions and relationships. The impact of touch is immediate and often subconscious, yet it can set the tone for an entire interaction. Consider the simple act of a handshake. This customary greeting in professional settings is more than just a formality. A firm, confident handshake can build trust and convey reliability, making a strong first impression. Conversely, a weak or hesitant handshake might suggest uncertainty or lack of confidence. Handshakes serve as an initial touchpoint that can shape the perception of the entire interaction.

In more personal settings, touch takes on a different significance. A pat on the back, for instance, can be incredibly comforting. It's a gesture that conveys support, encouragement, and empathy. When someone places a hand on your shoulder or gives you a gentle pat on the back, it can provide reassurance and a sense of connection. These small touches can strengthen bonds and show that you care, making the other person feel valued and understood. The power of touch lies in its ability to communicate emotions and intentions without words, creating a deeper, more intuitive connection.

The appropriateness of touch varies significantly depending on the context. In professional environments, touch should be limited and purposeful. Handshakes are a standard practice, and a light pat on the shoulder can be appropriate in some cases, such as offering congratulations or support. However, it's crucial to be mindful of personal boundaries and cultural norms to avoid making others uncomfortable. In contrast, personal settings often allow for more varied and frequent touch. Hugs, hand-holding, and even light touches on the arm or back are common ways to express affection and closeness. These gestures can enhance personal relationships and foster a sense of intimacy and trust.

Reading reactions to touch is essential for navigating social interactions effectively. Not everyone is comfortable with the same level of physical contact, and recognizing cues is key. If someone pulls away, tenses up, or shows signs of discomfort, it's a clear indication that they are not comfortable with the touch. Respecting these signals is crucial to maintaining a positive interaction and avoiding discomfort. On the other hand, positive reactions to touch, such as leaning in or relaxing, indicate that the person is comfortable and open to the interaction. Being attuned to these reactions helps you adjust your behavior to foster a more comfortable and respectful environment.

Cultural sensitivity in touch is another critical aspect to consider. Touch norms vary widely across cultures, and what is acceptable in one culture might be inappropriate in another. For example, hugging is a common greeting in many Latin cultures, signifying warmth and friendliness. In contrast, in many East Asian cultures, bowing is the preferred greeting, and physical touch, especially in initial interactions, might be considered intrusive. Adapting to these cultural expectations is vital to avoid misunderstandings and show respect. Understanding the cultural norms regarding touch can help you navigate cross-cultural interactions more effectively, ensuring that your gestures are received positively.

In professional settings, a firm handshake can convey confidence and establish trust right from the start. In more personal interactions, a hug or a gentle touch can communicate empathy and strengthen bonds. Recognizing and respecting others' comfort levels with touch is crucial for positive interactions. By being mindful of cultural norms and individual preferences, you can use touch to enhance your communication and build stronger, more meaningful connections in various aspects of your life.

Ending

Understanding the role of touch, along with other nonverbal cues like eye contact and personal space, equips you with the tools to navigate social and professional interactions more effectively. These skills form the foundation of successful communication, enabling you to connect with others on a deeper level. As we transition to the next chapter, we'll explore how to keep conversations engaging, ensuring that your interactions are not only meaningful but also enjoyable.

Chapter 4: Keeping Conversations Engaging

Imagine walking into a bustling room filled with chatter and laughter. You spot someone you recognize, but as you approach, you feel a familiar pang of anxiety. Your mind races, searching for the perfect way to break the ice. The importance of initiating a conversation can't be overstated. Icebreakers serve as the gateway to meaningful dialogue, breaking the initial barrier of silence that often keeps us from connecting with others. They set a friendly and open tone, inviting others to engage and share their stories.

Crafting Effective Icebreakers

Icebreakers are crucial for initiating conversations, especially in environments where people may not know each other well. They help to break the initial barrier of silence, making it easier to transition into more substantial topics. By setting a friendly and open tone, icebreakers create an atmosphere where everyone feels comfortable and willing to participate. Whether you're at a networking event, a business meeting, or a social gathering, the right icebreaker can pave the way for a rewarding conversation.

Different contexts call for different types of icebreakers. Environmental comments are a versatile and natural way to initiate dialogue. For instance, at a conference, you might say, "The keynote speaker was really inspiring, don't you think?" This type of comment is neutral and relevant to the setting, encouraging the other person to share their thoughts. Similarly, at a party, you could mention the music or the décor to kickstart the conversation. Noticing and commenting on your surroundings can provide an easy entry point into the conversation.

Shared experiences also make excellent icebreakers. Referring to a mutual situation or event creates an immediate connection and gives you a common ground to build upon. For example, if you and the other person attended the same workshop earlier, you might ask, "What did you think of the workshop on digital marketing?" This approach not only breaks the ice but also provides a topic for further discussion. Shared experiences give both parties a sense of familiarity and comfort, making it easier to engage in a meaningful conversation.

Crafting personalized icebreakers requires a bit of observation and creativity. Tailor your remarks to the individual by noticing details about them. If someone is wearing an interesting piece of jewelry, you could say, "I love your necklace! Where did you get it?" This type of comment shows that you are observant and genuinely interested, making the other person feel valued. Incorporating humor can also lighten the mood and make the interaction more enjoyable. A light-hearted joke or a playful comment about the situation can break down barriers and make the conversation flow more smoothly.

Specific examples of effective icebreakers can provide inspiration for your interactions. Compliments are always a good starting point. Saying something like, "I really like your shoes! They look so stylish," can make the other person feel good and open to talking. Food and drink are also reliable conversation starters. At a social event, you might ask, "Have you tried the appetizers here? They're amazing!" This not only breaks the ice but also gives you a topic to discuss further. The key is to be genuine and show interest in the other person.

Interactive Exercise: Icebreaker Brainstorm

Materials Needed:

- A notebook or a digital device for notes
- A timer

Steps:

1. Set a timer for 5 minutes.
2. Write down as many icebreaker ideas as you can think of.
3. Review your list and select your top three favorites.
4. Practice using these icebreakers in different social settings.

Effective icebreakers are essential tools for initiating and sustaining conversations. By understanding their importance, exploring different types, and crafting personalized remarks, you can navigate social and professional interactions with ease. These strategies will help you connect with others, build rapport, and keep conversations engaging.

4.2 The Secrets of Active Listening

Active listening is more than just hearing words; it's about fully concentrating on what the speaker is saying. This means giving them your undivided attention and showing genuine interest in their message. When you actively listen, you tune into the speaker's words, tone, and body language, ensuring that you truly understand their point of view. This level of engagement not only makes the other person feel valued but also enhances the quality of the conversation. In both personal and professional settings, mastering active listening can significantly improve your relationships and interactions.

One key technique for active listening is maintaining eye contact. This simple act signals to the speaker that you are focused and engaged. While maintaining eye contact, ensure your body language is open and receptive. Nod occasionally and use verbal affirmations like "I see" or "Interesting" to show that you are following along. These small gestures can make a big difference, as they encourage the speaker to continue sharing and reinforce their sense of being heard. Avoid crossing your arms or looking away, as these actions can suggest disinterest or distraction.

Reflective responses are another powerful tool in active listening. By paraphrasing the speaker's words, you demonstrate that you have not only heard but also understood their message. For example, if someone says, "I've been feeling overwhelmed at work," you might respond, "It sounds like your job has been quite demanding lately." This technique not only confirms your understanding but also encourages the speaker to elaborate further. Summarizing key points is equally important. At the end of a discussion, briefly recap the main ideas to ensure clarity and mutual understanding. This can help prevent misunderstandings and ensure that both parties are on the same page.

Avoiding common pitfalls is essential for effective active listening. One major mistake is interrupting the speaker. Interruptions can disrupt the flow of conversation and make the speaker feel undervalued. Instead, practice patience and allow the speaker to finish their thoughts before responding. Another common pitfall is allowing distractions to interfere with your listening. Whether it's your phone buzzing or your mind wandering, distractions can prevent you from fully engaging in the conversation. Make a conscious effort to minimize these interruptions by silencing your phone and focusing entirely on the speaker.

Interactive Exercise: Active Listening Practice

Materials Needed:

- A partner for conversation
- A quiet, distraction-free space

Steps:

1. Engage in a conversation with your partner on a chosen topic.
2. Practice maintaining eye contact, nodding, and using verbal affirmations.
3. Paraphrase and summarize key points during the conversation.
4. Reflect on your experience and discuss any challenges or improvements.

By integrating these techniques into your daily interactions, you can become a more effective and empathetic listener. Active listening not only enriches your conversations but also strengthens your connections with others. Whether you're in a business meeting, a casual chat with friends, or a family discussion, these skills can help you engage more deeply and meaningfully.

4.3 Utilizing Open-Ended Questions

Open-ended questions are incredibly effective tools for keeping conversations lively and engaging. Unlike closed questions, which can be answered with a simple "yes" or "no," open-ended questions encourage detailed responses and invite more depth and engagement. These types of questions signal to the other person that you are genuinely interested in their thoughts and experiences. They create a dialogue where both parties can explore various topics more thoroughly, making the conversation more enriching and dynamic. For instance, asking "What do you enjoy most about your job?" allows the other person to elaborate, share stories, and provide insights that can lead to a deeper connection.

Crafting effective open-ended questions requires a bit of thought and practice. Start your questions with words like "how," "what," "why," or "tell me about." These words naturally prompt the other person to provide more information. For example, instead of asking, "Did you have a good weekend?" which can be answered with a simple yes or no, ask, "What did you do over the weekend?" This small change in phrasing opens the door for the other person to share more about their experiences. Avoiding yes/no questions is key to promoting dialogue. Questions that require more than a one-word answer encourage the other person to think and engage more deeply in the conversation.

Specific examples of open-ended questions can be tailored to different contexts, making them versatile tools in any setting. In a professional environment, you might ask, "How did you get interested in your field?" This question not only shows interest in the other person's career but also provides an opportunity for them to share their journey and insights. In a social setting, you might ask, "What hobbies are you passionate about?" This invites the other person to talk about their interests and can lead to discovering common ground. Each open-ended question you ask should be designed to elicit thoughtful, detailed responses, making the conversation more enjoyable and meaningful for both parties.

Using follow-up questions is another effective way to keep the conversation flowing. Once the other person has answered an open-ended question, build on their response with additional questions that delve deeper into the topic. For example, if someone mentions they love hiking, you might follow up with, "That sounds interesting! What's your favorite trail, and why do you like it?" Asking for elaboration or examples shows that you are actively listening and interested in their experiences. It also provides more material for the conversation, keeping it engaging and dynamic.

Interactive Exercise: Open-Ended Questions Practice

Materials Needed:

- A notebook or a digital device for notes
- A timer

Steps:

1. Set a timer for 5 minutes.
2. Write down as many open-ended questions as you can think of.
3. Review your list and select your top three favorites.
4. Practice using these questions in different social and professional settings.

By incorporating open-ended questions into your conversations, you can transform ordinary interactions into engaging dialogues. These questions encourage others to share more about themselves, making the conversation richer and more meaningful. Whether you're at a business meeting, a social event, or a casual get-together, open-ended questions can help you connect with others on a deeper level and keep the conversation flowing naturally.

4.4 Mastering the Art of Storytelling

Storytelling is a powerful tool that can transform ordinary conversations into memorable and engaging dialogues. When you weave a story into your conversation, you make your message more relatable and memorable. Stories connect with people on an emotional level, making abstract concepts tangible and personal. Think about a time when someone told you a compelling story. You probably remember the details and emotions better than if they had simply stated facts. This emotional connection is what makes storytelling so effective in engaging your audience.

To craft a good story, you need to understand its key components. Setting the scene with context and background is crucial. Imagine you're describing a memorable vacation. Instead of saying, "I went to Italy," you might start with, "It was a warm summer evening in Tuscany, and the air was filled with the scent of blooming jasmine." This vivid description immediately transports the listener into your experience. Next, build a narrative arc with a clear beginning, middle, and end. Your story should have a logical flow that keeps your listener engaged. For instance, you could describe the anticipation before your trip, the adventures you had, and the lessons you learned along the way.

Effective storytelling also involves using vivid, sensory details to paint a picture. Describe the sights, sounds, and feelings to make the story come alive. If you're recounting a funny incident, mention the expressions on people's faces, the sounds of laughter, and how it felt to be in that moment. Incorporating humor can also make your stories more relatable and enjoyable. People love to laugh, and a well-placed joke or a humorous twist can make your story stand out. Relatable experiences are another key element. Share stories that your audience can connect with, whether it's a common work challenge or a universal life experience. This makes your story more impactful and engaging.

Practicing storytelling is essential to mastering this skill. Start by sharing personal anecdotes in casual settings. These low-pressure environments are perfect for honing your storytelling abilities. Pay attention to your audience's reactions and adjust your story accordingly. Another effective practice method is rehearsing stories before networking events. Think of a few key stories that highlight your experiences and skills. Practice telling them in a way that is engaging and concise. This preparation will make you more confident and ready to share your stories when the opportunity arises.

Interactive Exercise: Storytelling Practice

Materials Needed:

- A notebook or a digital device for notes
- A quiet space

Steps:

1. Write down a memorable experience you've had.
2. Break it down into three parts: beginning, middle, and end.
3. Add vivid, sensory details to each part.
4. Practice telling the story out loud.

By incorporating storytelling into your conversations, you can make your interactions more engaging and memorable. This technique allows you to connect with others on a deeper level, making your message more impactful. Whether you're in a professional setting, a social event, or a casual chat, storytelling can elevate your communication skills and leave a lasting impression.

4.5 Techniques for Handling Awkward Silences

Awkward silences happen to everyone. They can occur naturally in conversations as people pause to think, but sometimes these pauses become uncomfortable gaps that make both parties feel uneasy. Understanding why these silences happen is the first step in handling them effectively. Natural pauses are a normal part of any dialogue, giving participants time to process information or consider their responses. However, when these pauses stretch too long, they can become awkward. The psychological impact of silence in social interactions is significant. People may feel judged, rejected, or simply unsure of what to say next, which can make the conversation feel strained.

To prevent these uncomfortable gaps, it's helpful to prepare in advance. Having a mental list of potential topics can save you from scrambling for words when the conversation lulls. Think about subjects that are universally interesting or relevant to the setting you're in. For example, if you're at a professional event, you might prepare to discuss recent industry news, while at a social gathering, you could consider talking about popular movies or sports. Using humor is another effective strategy. A light-hearted joke or a playful comment about the situation can break the tension and get the conversation back on track.

When a silence does occur, how you handle it can make all the difference. Acknowledging the pause with a light comment can ease the tension. You might say, "It looks like we both need a moment to think!" This shows that you are aware of the silence and are comfortable with it, which can help the other person feel more at ease. Another approach is to smoothly transition to a new topic. Asking a question or introducing a new subject can reignite the dialogue. For instance, you could say, "By the way, have you heard about the new restaurant that just opened downtown?" This technique not only fills the silence but also directs the conversation in a new and interesting direction.

Specific conversation starters can be lifesavers in these moments. Phrases like "This reminds me of…" can seamlessly introduce a related topic, keeping the flow of conversation natural. For example, if you're discussing travel and hit a silence, you might say, "This reminds me of a trip I took to Italy last summer. Have you ever been?" Another useful phrase is "By the way, have you heard about…?" This can introduce a current event or interesting fact that shifts the conversation smoothly. For instance, "By the way, have you heard about the new technology they're using in medical research?" These phrases not only fill the silence but also invite the other person to share their thoughts, keeping the conversation engaging.

Handling awkward silences effectively requires a mix of preparation, awareness, and quick thinking. By understanding the reasons behind these pauses and having a few strategies up your sleeve, you can navigate them with confidence. Whether you're in a professional setting, a social event, or a casual conversation, these techniques can help you keep the dialogue flowing smoothly and make your interactions more enjoyable.

Chapter 5: Navigating Difficult Conversations

Imagine standing on the edge of a cliff, the ground beneath you crumbling, and the chasm of a difficult conversation yawning wide before you. Your heart races, palms sweat, and thoughts swirl in a chaotic dance of anxiety and dread. Difficult conversations—whether with a colleague, a loved one, or even a stranger—often evoke this kind of visceral reaction. Yet, these conversations are inevitable and necessary for growth and resolution. The key to navigating them successfully lies in preparation.

5.1 Preparing for Tough Conversations

Understanding the importance of preparation is the first step in transforming anxiety into confidence. Preparation is crucial because it reduces uncertainty and helps you approach the conversation with a clear mind. When you plan, you can anticipate potential challenges and devise strategies to address them. This foresight can significantly reduce anxiety, allowing you to focus on the conversation itself rather than getting lost in a sea of worries. Clarifying your objectives and desired outcomes is equally important. Knowing what you want to achieve helps you stay on track and ensures that the conversation is productive. For instance, if you're addressing a performance issue with a team member, your objective might be to provide constructive feedback that leads to improvement, rather than simply expressing frustration.

Gathering necessary information is another vital aspect of preparation. Before entering a difficult conversation, arm yourself with relevant facts and data. This foundation allows you to present your points logically and persuasively. For example, if you're discussing a missed deadline with a colleague, have the project timeline and specific details at hand. This approach not only strengthens your position but also demonstrates that you are well-informed. Additionally, understanding the other person's perspective can make a significant difference. Take the time to consider their viewpoint and gather any information that might help you empathize with their situation. This empathetic approach can create a more collaborative atmosphere and increase the chances of a positive outcome.

Setting the right environment is crucial for the success of a difficult conversation. Choosing a private and neutral location can make both parties feel more comfortable and less defensive. A quiet room free from distractions allows you to maintain focus and ensures that the conversation remains confidential. For example, if you're discussing a sensitive issue with a coworker, booking a private meeting room can provide the necessary privacy. Minimizing distractions, such as turning off your phone and closing the door, helps create an environment conducive to open and honest dialogue. This setting signals respect for the conversation and the person you're speaking with, fostering a sense of safety and trust.

Practicing the conversation can significantly improve your confidence and effectiveness. Role-playing with a trusted friend or colleague allows you to rehearse your points and receive feedback. This practice can help you refine your approach and anticipate potential responses. For instance, if you're preparing to discuss a conflict with a team member, role-playing can help you practice staying calm and focused, even if the other person becomes defensive. Visualizing different scenarios and responses is another powerful technique. Take a few moments to imagine various outcomes and how you might handle them. This mental rehearsal can help you feel more prepared and adaptable, reducing the likelihood of being caught off guard.

Interactive Exercise: Conversation Rehearsal

Materials Needed:

- A trusted friend or colleague
- A quiet, private space

Steps:

1. Explain the context of the conversation to your partner.
2. Role-play the conversation, taking turns to play both roles.
3. Provide feedback to each other on what worked well and what could be improved.
4. Repeat the exercise, incorporating the feedback to refine your approach.

By focusing on these aspects of preparation, you can approach difficult conversations with greater confidence and clarity. Reducing anxiety through planning, gathering necessary information, setting the right environment, and practicing the conversation are all essential steps. These strategies not only improve your ability to navigate tough discussions but also increase the likelihood of achieving a positive and productive outcome.

Staying Calm Under Pressure

Navigating tough conversations requires a calm and composed demeanor, yet staying calm under pressure can often seem like an insurmountable challenge. The first step is recognizing your emotional triggers. Common triggers in difficult conversations can include feeling misunderstood, disrespected, or unfairly treated. Identifying these triggers involves a degree of self-awareness, which can be developed through reflection and mindfulness. Pay attention to what causes your heart rate to spike or your palms to sweat. Is it a particular word, tone, or topic? Once you've pinpointed your triggers, you can devise strategies to manage them. Self-awareness techniques, such as keeping a journal of your emotional responses, can help you understand and predict your reactions, allowing you to prepare better for future conversations.

Breathing and relaxation techniques are invaluable tools for staying calm physically and mentally. Deep breathing exercises can help reduce stress by lowering your heart rate and calming your nervous system. Try the 4-7-8 technique: inhale through your nose for four seconds, hold your breath for seven seconds, and exhale through your mouth for eight seconds. This method can quickly bring a sense of calm and focus. Progressive muscle relaxation is another effective technique. It involves tensing and then slowly relaxing different muscle groups in your body, starting from your toes and working your way up to your head. This practice not only helps reduce physical tension but also shifts your focus away from stress-inducing thoughts, allowing you to maintain your composure during the conversation.

Staying focused and present during a tough conversation is essential for effective communication. Mindfulness techniques can help you stay grounded and attentive. One simple practice is to focus on your breath, bringing your attention back to the present moment whenever your mind starts to wander. This can prevent you from getting lost in anxious thoughts or distractions. Avoiding distractions is equally important. Choose a quiet environment, put away your phone, and make a conscious effort to stay engaged in the conversation. Staying on topic can also help maintain focus. If the discussion starts to veer off course, gently steer it back by saying something like, "Let's get back to the main issue at hand." This not only keeps the conversation productive but also shows respect for the other person's time and concerns.

Positive self-talk is a powerful tool for maintaining composure and confidence during difficult conversations. Affirmations can help you stay calm and centered. Before the conversation, remind yourself of positive statements like, "I can handle this," or "I am prepared and capable." During the conversation, if you start to feel overwhelmed, silently repeat these affirmations to yourself. Reframing negative thoughts into positive ones can also make a significant difference. Instead of thinking, "This is going to be a disaster," tell yourself, "This is an opportunity to resolve an issue and improve our relationship." This shift in perspective can reduce anxiety and help you approach the conversation with a more positive and proactive mindset.

Interactive Exercise: Positive Self-Talk Practice

Materials Needed:

- A notebook or a digital device for notes

Steps:

1. Write down three affirmations that resonate with you and make you feel confident.
2. Reflect on a recent difficult conversation and identify any negative thoughts you had.

3. Reframe those negative thoughts into positive ones.
4. Practice using these affirmations and positive reframes in your daily life to build the habit.

Recognizing your triggers, practicing breathing and relaxation techniques, staying focused and present, and using positive self-talk are all essential strategies for staying calm under pressure. These techniques not only help you maintain your composure but also enhance your ability to communicate effectively and navigate difficult conversations successfully. By integrating these practices into your daily routine, you can develop greater resilience and confidence, making it easier to handle challenging interactions with poise.

Techniques for Conflict Resolution

Understanding the nature of conflict is the first step towards resolution. Conflicts often arise from miscommunication and misunderstandings, where messages are interpreted differently from what was intended. For instance, an email's tone might be perceived as harsh when the sender meant to be direct. Differences in values, goals, or interests can also spark conflict. One person might prioritize teamwork, while another values individual achievement. These differences can lead to clashes if not addressed.

Active listening and empathy are crucial in resolving conflicts. Reflective listening, where you paraphrase what the other person has said, shows that you understand their point of view. For example, if a colleague expresses frustration about workload, you might say, "It sounds like you're feeling overwhelmed by the current projects." This not only validates their feelings but also opens the door for further dialogue. Empathy goes a step further by allowing you to feel what the other person is experiencing. Imagine yourself in their shoes, and consider how you would feel in their situation. This approach fosters a deeper connection and can soften the tension.

Finding common ground is another effective strategy for conflict resolution. By identifying shared interests and goals, you can shift the focus from differences to mutual benefits. Asking open-ended questions can help uncover these commonalities. Questions like "What outcomes are you hoping for?" or "How can we work together to achieve our goals?" encourage the other person to share their perspective and can reveal areas of agreement. Focusing on mutual benefits and solutions rather than individual grievances can transform a contentious discussion into a collaborative effort. This shift in focus can pave the way for a more constructive dialogue, where both parties feel heard and valued.

Collaborative problem-solving is the cornerstone of effective conflict resolution. This approach involves working together to find a solution that satisfies both parties. Start by brainstorming potential solutions, encouraging everyone involved to share their ideas. This process can generate a range of options and foster a sense of ownership over the resolution. Once you have a list of possible solutions, evaluate them together, considering the pros and cons of each. This collaborative evaluation ensures that all perspectives are considered and increases the likelihood of finding a mutually acceptable solution. Finally, agree on a course of action and outline the steps needed to implement it. This clear plan of action ensures accountability and helps prevent future conflicts.

Understanding the nature of conflict, practicing active listening and empathy, finding common ground, and engaging in collaborative problem-solving are key techniques for resolving conflicts effectively. By applying these strategies, you can navigate conflicts with confidence and foster more positive and productive relationships.

5.4 Delivering Critical Feedback Constructively

Constructive feedback is vital for growth and development, both personally and professionally. It encourages improvement without causing defensiveness and helps maintain positive relationships. When delivered effectively, feedback can be a powerful tool for change, allowing individuals to recognize areas for improvement while feeling supported and valued. This balance is crucial because feedback that feels like an attack can lead to resistance and resentment, undermining the very goals it's meant to achieve. Instead, feedback should be seen as a collaborative effort to foster better performance and stronger relationships.

One effective technique for delivering constructive feedback is the "sandwich" method, which involves sandwiching criticism between positive comments. Start with positive feedback to set a supportive tone. For instance, if you're giving feedback to a colleague, you might begin by saying, "I really appreciate your dedication to the project; your hard work has made a big difference." This opening makes the recipient more receptive to hearing about areas for improvement. Next, address the areas that need improvement. Be specific and objective, providing concrete examples. You might say, "However, I've noticed that there have been some delays in meeting deadlines. For example, the last report was submitted two days late, which affected the team's schedule." Finally, end with encouragement and support, reinforcing your commitment to their success. You could conclude with, "I believe you have the skills to manage your time more effectively, and I'm here to help if you need any support."

Being specific and objective in your feedback is essential. Vague or general statements can be confusing and unhelpful. Instead, provide concrete examples and evidence to illustrate your points. For instance, rather than saying, "Your work needs improvement," specify the areas that require attention, such as, "The recent presentation lacked detailed data analysis, which is crucial for our client reports." This clarity helps the recipient understand exactly what needs to change and why. Avoiding vague statements ensures that your feedback is actionable and focused, making it easier for the recipient to implement the necessary changes.

Offering solutions and support is another critical aspect of delivering constructive feedback. Suggest actionable steps for improvement, providing clear guidance on how to address the issues. For example, you might say, "To improve the quality of your reports, consider dedicating an extra hour to data analysis and double-checking your sources." Offering resources or assistance can also be incredibly helpful. You might suggest relevant training programs, recommend useful tools, or offer to mentor them through the process. This support not only makes the feedback more constructive but also demonstrates your investment in their growth and development.

Case Study: Effective Feedback in Action

Consider the case of a sales manager who noticed that one of their team members, Sarah, was struggling with closing deals. Instead of simply pointing out her shortcomings, the manager decided to use the "sandwich" method. They started by acknowledging Sarah's strengths, saying, "Sarah, your enthusiasm and energy in client meetings are impressive and create a positive atmosphere." Then, they addressed the specific issue, "However, I've noticed that some deals are falling through at the final stage. For instance, last week's deal with XYZ Corp didn't close because the proposal lacked detailed pricing information." Finally, they offered a solution and support, "I think spending some time on refining your proposals could help. Let's set aside some time to go over your next proposal together." This approach made Sarah feel valued and supported, and she was able to improve her closing rate significantly.

Delivering feedback constructively requires a balance of honesty, empathy, and support. By using techniques like the "sandwich" method, being specific and objective, and offering solutions and support, you can help others improve without causing defensiveness. This approach not only fosters growth and development but also strengthens relationships, creating a positive and collaborative environment.

5.5 Apologizing Effectively and Sincerely

The power of a sincere apology cannot be underestimated. When you offer a genuine apology, you acknowledge your mistakes and take responsibility for your actions. This act of humility helps rebuild trust and respect, both essential for mending and strengthening relationships. Whether it's a minor misunderstanding with a friend or a significant error at work, a heartfelt apology can pave the way for healing and reconciliation. By owning up to your mistakes, you show maturity and integrity, qualities that can enhance your credibility and deepen your connections with others.

Components of a genuine apology are straightforward but crucial. First, express regret and acknowledge the harm caused. Saying, "I regret that my actions hurt you," shows that you understand the impact of your behavior. Next, take responsibility without making excuses. Avoid statements like, "I'm sorry, but I was stressed." Instead, say, "I'm sorry for my actions and the impact they had on you." Finally, offer to make amends. This could involve correcting the mistake, making reparations, or simply asking, "How can I make this right?" These elements together demonstrate that you are committed to repairing the harm and preventing future issues.

Avoiding common pitfalls is crucial for an effective apology. Conditional apologies, such as "I'm sorry if you were offended," can come across as insincere and deflective. They imply that the other person's feelings are the problem rather than your actions. Instead, be direct and clear about what you're apologizing for. Another mistake is deflecting blame. Saying, "I'm sorry, but you also..." shifts responsibility and can escalate the conflict. Focus solely on your actions, acknowledging them without bringing in the other person's behavior. This approach shows that you are willing to take full responsibility, which can help de-escalate the situation.

Practicing apology scripts can prepare you for real-life situations. Consider these examples. Apologizing to a friend for a misunderstanding might sound like, "I'm really sorry for the misunderstanding we had yesterday. I didn't mean to dismiss your feelings, and I regret that my words caused you pain. Can we talk about how to move forward?" This script acknowledges the harm, takes responsibility, and seeks a way to repair the relationship. For a work error, you might say, "I apologize for the mistake in the report. It was my responsibility, and I understand the inconvenience it caused the team. I've already taken steps to correct it and ensure it doesn't happen again." This approach not only acknowledges the error but also demonstrates your commitment to improvement.

Interactive Exercise: Apology Practice

1. **Scenario 1 - Friend**: "I'm really sorry for the misunderstanding we had yesterday. I didn't mean to dismiss your feelings, and I regret that my words caused you pain. Can we talk about how to move forward?"
2. **Scenario 2 - Colleague**: "I apologize for the mistake in the report. It was my responsibility, and I understand the inconvenience it caused the team. I've already taken steps to correct it and ensure it doesn't happen again."

In both scenarios, the structure remains consistent: express regret, take responsibility, and offer a way to make amends. Practicing these scripts can help you internalize the components of a genuine apology, making it easier to respond appropriately in the moment. Remember, the goal of an apology is not just to say the right words but to genuinely communicate your remorse and commitment to making things right. This sincerity can go a long way in repairing relationships and building trust.

By focusing on sincere, well-structured apologies, you can navigate difficult conversations more effectively, whether in personal or professional settings. A genuine apology acknowledges mistakes, takes responsibility, and seeks to make amends, fostering trust and respect. Practicing these skills can help you respond appropriately in real-life situations, strengthening your relationships and enhancing your communication skills.

5.6 Navigating Emotional Conversations

Navigating emotional conversations requires a keen sense of awareness and empathy. Recognizing emotional cues is the first step in understanding how the other person feels. Body language and facial expressions are powerful indicators of emotion. For instance, crossed arms may signal defensiveness, while a furrowed brow might indicate confusion or concern. Paying attention to these non-verbal signals allows you to respond more effectively. Facial expressions such as a smile can convey openness and warmth, while a clenched jaw might reveal tension or anger. By tuning into these cues, you can gauge the emotional state of the person you're speaking with, which helps you tailor your responses accordingly.

Listening for emotional undertones in speech is equally important. The tone, pitch, and pace of someone's voice often reveal more than their words. A raised voice may indicate frustration or anger, while a trembling voice might signal fear or sadness. By focusing on these vocal cues, you can better understand the underlying emotions driving the conversation. For example, if someone speaks quickly and with a high pitch, they may be anxious or excited. Slower, softer speech might suggest they are feeling overwhelmed or introspective. Being attuned to these subtleties helps you respond with greater empathy and understanding.

Managing your own emotions during an emotional conversation is crucial for maintaining composure and effectiveness. Practicing emotional regulation techniques can help you stay calm and focused. One effective method is to take deep breaths, which can slow your heart rate and help you regain control. If emotions become overwhelming, don't hesitate to take a break. A brief pause allows you to collect your thoughts and return to the conversation with a clearer mind. For instance, you might say, "I need a moment to gather my thoughts," giving yourself the space to process your emotions. This pause can prevent you from reacting impulsively and ensure that your response is measured and thoughtful.

Responding empathetically to others' emotions is essential for building trust and rapport. Using validating statements shows that you understand and accept the other person's feelings. Phrases like, "I can see why you feel that way," or "That sounds really tough," can make the other person feel heard and supported. Offering support and reassurance further strengthens this bond. For example, you might say, "I'm here for you, and we'll work through this together." These responses not only validate the other person's emotions but also provide a sense of comfort and solidarity. By showing empathy, you create a safe space for open and honest dialogue.

Ending an emotional conversation on a positive note is vital for maintaining the relationship and ensuring that both parties feel valued. Summarizing key points and agreements helps clarify what was discussed and ensures that everyone is on the same page. For instance, you might say, "So, we've agreed to set up regular check-ins to address any concerns moving forward." This recap reinforces the commitments made during the conversation and provides a clear path forward. Expressing appreciation for the other person's openness is also important. A simple statement like, "Thank you for sharing your feelings with me," can go a long way in reinforcing mutual respect and understanding.

Navigating emotional conversations effectively involves recognizing and responding to emotional cues, managing your own emotions, and showing empathy towards others. By focusing on these aspects, you can create a more supportive and understanding environment, fostering stronger connections and resolving conflicts more effectively.

Ending

Emotional conversations are inevitable, but handling them with care can lead to deeper understanding and stronger relationships. By recognizing emotional cues, managing your own reactions, and responding empathetically, you can navigate these challenging discussions with grace and efficacy. As we move forward, we will explore strategies for building genuine connections in various social and professional settings, enhancing your ability to communicate with anyone, anywhere.

Dear Reader,

Thank you for choosing *How to Talk to Anyone*! We hope you're finding the insights and strategies useful so far. As you're progressing through the book, we'd love to hear your thoughts!

Your feedback at this stage can help us understand how the content resonates with you. Whether you're finding certain sections particularly helpful, or you have suggestions for improvement, we'd love to hear from you!

Your input will help us ensure that *How to Talk to Anyone* meets your expectations and continues to provide value.

How to Leave Your Review: Please take a moment to share your thoughts by leaving a review on the platform (Amazon) or by clicking on the link below.

https://www.amazon.com/How-talk-anyone-ebook/dp/B0DHPSX68S/

Thank you for your time, and we look forward to hearing your feedback!

Best regards,

Debra Miller

Chapter 6: Effective Networking Strategies

Think back to the last time you attended a networking event. Perhaps it was a bustling conference hall filled with energetic conversations, or a more intimate business mixer with a handful of professionals. As you navigated the room, you noticed some people making connections effortlessly while others seemed unsure how to approach a conversation. This scene is all too familiar for many of us. Networking, while essential for career and personal growth, can often feel daunting. Yet, with the right strategies, you can turn these interactions into valuable opportunities.

Crafting a Memorable Elevator Pitch

Understanding the Purpose of an Elevator Pitch

An elevator pitch is your golden ticket in the networking world. Imagine you have just 30 seconds in an elevator with a potential client, employer, or partner. How do you capture their attention and make a lasting impression? A well-crafted elevator pitch is concise and compelling, designed to spark interest and encourage further conversation. Its primary purpose is not to close a deal but to pique curiosity and earn you more time to discuss your ideas or services. Capturing attention quickly is crucial because, in today's fast-paced world, people have limited time and a plethora of distractions. Your pitch needs to stand out and make them want to know more. Making a strong first impression can set the tone for a productive relationship, whether professional or personal.

Key Components of an Effective Elevator Pitch

To create an effective elevator pitch, you need to focus on three key components: introduction, value proposition, and call to action. Start with a brief introduction that clearly states who you are and what you do. For example, "Hi, I'm Debra Miller, and I specialize in real estate finance." This opening provides essential context and sets the stage for the rest of your pitch. Next, move on to your value proposition. This is where you explain what sets you apart from others in your field and how you can bring value to the person you're speaking to. For instance, "I help clients secure financing for their dream homes by leveraging my extensive experience in banking and finance." This statement highlights your unique strengths and the benefits you offer. Finally, include a call to action. This should encourage the other person to continue the conversation or take the next step. You might say, "I'd love to discuss how my services can help you achieve your financial goals. Can we schedule a time to chat further?"

Tailoring Your Pitch to Different Audiences

Customizing your pitch based on your audience is key to making it effective. Adapting your language and tone for different industries ensures that your message resonates with the listener. For example, when speaking to tech professionals, you might emphasize your expertise in leveraging financial technology to streamline processes. On the other hand, when addressing a group of entrepreneurs, you could focus on how your services can help them grow their businesses. Highlighting relevant skills and experiences is crucial. Consider what matters most to the person you're speaking to and tailor your pitch accordingly. If you're at a job fair, emphasize your qualifications and how they align with the company's needs. At a networking event for small business owners, focus on how your expertise can solve common challenges they face. This targeted approach makes your pitch more engaging and relevant, increasing the likelihood of a positive response.

Practicing Your Pitch

To perfect your pitch, practice is essential. Rehearse with friends or colleagues to gain feedback and refine your delivery. This practice helps you become more comfortable and confident, making your pitch more natural and compelling. Recording and reviewing your pitch can also be incredibly beneficial. Listen to your tone, pace, and clarity, and make adjustments as needed. You might notice areas where you can be more concise or where your enthusiasm could be more evident. Consistent practice ensures that your pitch flows smoothly and effectively, even in high-pressure situations.

Interactive Exercise: Crafting and Practicing Your Elevator Pitch

Materials Needed:

- A notebook or digital device for notes
- A recording device (your phone will do)

Steps:

1. Write down a draft of your elevator pitch, focusing on the three key components: introduction, value proposition, and call to action.
2. Practice delivering your pitch out loud, paying attention to your tone and pace.
3. Record yourself and review the recording. Note any areas for improvement.

4. Make necessary adjustments and practice again until you feel confident.

By crafting a memorable elevator pitch and tailoring it to your audience, you can capture attention quickly and make a strong first impression. This strategy is vital for effective networking, whether you're meeting new people at a business event, a social gathering, or even an impromptu encounter in an elevator.

Strategies for Following Up After Networking Events

The Importance of Following Up

Imagine you've just returned from a bustling networking event. You've collected a stack of business cards and made several promising connections. The initial interaction is only the beginning. Following up in a timely manner is crucial for building and maintaining those relationships. Reinforcing initial connections shows that you are serious about fostering a professional relationship. It demonstrates that you were paying attention and value the interaction. Timely follow-up also showcases your professionalism and interest, setting you apart from those who might let the opportunity slip away.

Crafting Effective Follow-Up Messages

When it comes to crafting follow-up messages, personalization is key. Start by referencing specific points from your conversation. This demonstrates that you were engaged and attentive. For example, "It was great to hear about your innovative project on renewable energy at the conference." This not only jogs the recipient's memory but also makes the message feel more personal. Expressing gratitude for the interaction is equally important. A simple, "Thank you for taking the time to chat with me," goes a long way in showing appreciation. Keep your message concise and relevant. Avoid generic statements and focus on what makes your connection unique.

Timing Your Follow-Ups

Timing is everything when it comes to follow-ups. Sending your follow-up message within 24 to 48 hours of the event is optimal. This ensures that the interaction is still fresh in both your minds. It also shows that you are proactive and eager to maintain the connection. If you wait too long, the initial connection may weaken, and the impact of your message diminishes. Additionally, scheduling reminders for subsequent follow-ups can help keep the relationship alive. A brief check-in a few weeks later, or a note during a relevant holiday or event, can reinforce your commitment to the relationship.

Using Multiple Follow-Up Channels

Using various communication methods can enhance your follow-up efforts. Email is a common and effective choice, allowing you to provide detailed information and maintain a professional tone. Phone calls add a personal touch and can be more immediate. Social media platforms, particularly LinkedIn, are excellent for staying connected and engaging with your new contact's content. Commenting on their posts or sharing relevant articles can keep you on their radar. Handwritten notes are another powerful tool. They add a personal touch that stands out in today's digital age. A brief, sincere note can leave a lasting impression and show that you put in extra effort to make the connection meaningful.

Interactive Exercise: Crafting Your Follow-Up Message

Materials Needed:

- A notebook or digital device for notes

Steps:

1. Write a draft of your follow-up message, including specific points from your conversation and a note of gratitude.
2. Review and edit the message to ensure it is concise and personalized.
3. Decide on the best follow-up channel (email, phone, social media, handwritten note).
4. Send the message within 24-48 hours of the initial interaction.

By following up promptly and thoughtfully, you can turn initial contacts into valuable relationships. This strategy not only reinforces connections but also demonstrates your professionalism and genuine interest in building a network.

Building a Professional Network from Scratch

Starting from scratch to build a professional network can feel like a daunting task, but it's entirely achievable with the right approach. The first step is identifying networking opportunities where you can meet like-minded professionals and potential collaborators. Industry conferences and trade shows are prime venues. These events gather experts and enthusiasts from a specific field, making them fertile ground for meaningful connections. Attending these events not only exposes you to the latest trends and developments but also provides ample opportunities to engage in conversations with industry leaders and peers. Look for events that align with your professional interests and make a point to attend them regularly.

Professional associations and meetups are equally valuable. Joining an association related to your field can provide access to exclusive events, webinars, and networking opportunities. These organizations often host regular meetings and conferences, offering a structured environment to meet new contacts. Similarly, local meetups focused on specific industries or interests can be a great way to expand your network in a more casual setting. Websites like Meetup.com can help you find groups that match your interests. By actively participating in these gatherings, you can build a network of contacts who share your professional passions and goals.

Approaching new contacts at these events requires a mix of confidence and strategy. Introducing yourself confidently sets the tone for a positive interaction. A firm handshake, a warm smile, and a clear introduction can make a strong first impression. For instance, you might say, "Hi, I'm Debra Miller. I work in real estate finance and specialize in helping clients secure funding for their dream homes." This concise introduction provides key information about who you are and what you do, making it easier for the other person to engage with you. Asking insightful questions about their work can further build rapport. Questions like, "What inspired you to enter this field?" or "What challenges are you currently facing in your projects?" show genuine interest and encourage the other person to share their experiences. This approach not only fosters a meaningful conversation but also helps you gather valuable insights and establish a connection.

Maintaining a networking log is a practical way to keep track of your interactions and follow-ups. After each event, take a few minutes to jot down the contact details of the people you met, along with key points discussed. This log can include names, job titles, companies, and any memorable elements of your conversation. Setting reminders for follow-ups and check-ins is also crucial. Whether it's a quick email to say, "It was great meeting you at the conference," or a reminder to touch base in a few months, these actions show that you value the connection and are committed to nurturing it. Over time, this log becomes a valuable resource, helping you stay organized and proactive in your networking efforts.

Expanding your network strategically involves leveraging existing connections for introductions. If you know someone who is well-connected in your industry, don't hesitate to ask for an introduction to people you want to meet. A warm introduction from a mutual contact can significantly increase your chances of building a meaningful connection. Additionally, joining online communities and forums can extend your reach beyond physical events. Platforms like LinkedIn offer various groups and forums where professionals discuss industry trends, share insights, and network. Engaging in these online spaces by participating in discussions, sharing articles, and connecting with other members can help you build a robust network. These interactions can lead to new opportunities, collaborations, and valuable knowledge sharing.

Building a professional network from scratch requires a proactive and strategic approach. By identifying the right networking opportunities, confidently approaching new contacts, maintaining a detailed networking log, and expanding your network through existing connections and online communities, you can create a strong and supportive professional network. This network not only provides valuable resources and opportunities but also fosters personal and professional growth.

Leveraging Social Media for Networking

Choosing the right social media platforms can significantly impact your professional networking efforts. LinkedIn stands out as the premier platform for industry-specific connections. It offers a space where professionals from various fields come together to share insights, discuss trends, and build relationships. LinkedIn allows you to join industry-specific groups, participate in discussions, and connect with thought leaders. This platform is particularly beneficial for those looking to establish themselves within their field, as it provides ample opportunities to showcase your expertise and engage with a targeted audience. On LinkedIn, you can easily connect with colleagues, potential clients, and industry influencers, making it a powerful tool for expanding your professional network.

Twitter, on the other hand, serves as an excellent platform for thought leadership and engagement. With its fast-paced nature, Twitter allows you to share real-time updates, industry news, and insights. Participating in Twitter chats and using relevant hashtags can help you join conversations related to your field. This platform is ideal for staying updated on the latest trends and connecting with industry leaders. By engaging with their tweets, you can build rapport and establish yourself as a knowledgeable and active participant in your industry. Twitter's concise format encourages you to share valuable content succinctly, making it easier to capture attention and foster engagement.

Creating a professional online presence is crucial for effective networking on social media. Start by crafting a compelling LinkedIn summary that clearly communicates who you are, what you do, and what you offer. This summary should highlight your key achievements, skills, and professional goals. Use a conversational tone to make it relatable and engaging. Additionally, ensure that your profile picture is professional and up-to-date. A high-quality photo where you are dressed appropriately for your industry can make a significant difference in how you are perceived. Remember, your online profile is often the first impression others have of you, so make it count.

Engaging with content on social media is another critical aspect of building your network. Actively participate in online discussions by commenting on industry articles and posts. Share your insights, ask questions, and offer thoughtful feedback. This not only demonstrates your expertise but also shows that you are engaged and interested in the field. Sharing valuable content and insights can further enhance your online presence. Curate and share articles, reports, and other resources that are relevant to your industry. Adding your commentary or perspective can make your shares more impactful and encourage others to engage with you. This consistent engagement helps you stay visible and relevant in your professional community.

Reaching out to potential contacts on social media requires a strategic approach. Sending personalized connection requests is a good starting point. Instead of using the default message, take a few moments to craft a personalized note that explains why you want to connect. Mention any mutual connections, shared interests, or recent interactions. For example, "Hi [Name], I enjoyed your recent article on sustainable business practices. I would love to connect and discuss further." This personalized approach increases the likelihood of your connection request being accepted. Engaging through direct messages is another effective strategy. Once your connection request is accepted, follow up with a message that continues the conversation. Ask questions, share relevant resources, or suggest a virtual coffee chat. This proactive engagement helps build a stronger relationship and opens the door for future collaborations.

Interactive Exercise: Optimizing Your LinkedIn Profile

Materials Needed:

- A LinkedIn account

Steps:

1. Review your current LinkedIn profile and note areas for improvement.
2. Update your summary to reflect your current skills, achievements, and professional goals.
3. Ensure your profile picture is professional and up-to-date.
4. Engage with at least three posts by commenting and sharing your insights.

By leveraging social media platforms like LinkedIn and Twitter effectively, you can enhance your professional networking efforts. Creating a compelling online presence, engaging with content, and reaching out to potential contacts strategically can help you build a robust network. These steps not only expand your reach but also establish you as a credible and active participant in your industry.

Networking for Introverts: Overcoming Challenges

Networking can feel like a daunting task, especially if you're an introvert. However, introverts often possess unique strengths that can be incredibly advantageous in building meaningful connections. One of the most valuable skills you bring to the table is deep listening. Unlike more extroverted individuals who may dominate conversations, you have the ability to truly hear what others are saying. This skill allows you to pick up on subtle cues and nuances, making others feel understood and valued. Thoughtful and meaningful interactions are another hallmark of introverts. You tend to engage in conversations that go beyond small talk, delving into topics that matter. This depth can create stronger, more lasting connections.

When preparing for networking events, setting specific goals can make a significant difference in how comfortable and confident you feel. Instead of approaching the event with the vague aim of "meeting people," set clear, achievable objectives. Perhaps you want to connect with three new individuals or gather information about a particular industry trend. Having these goals in mind gives you a sense of purpose and direction. Practicing conversation starters in advance can also ease the anxiety of initiating interactions. Think about a few opening lines or questions you can use to break the ice. For instance, "What brought you to this event?" or "Have you attended this conference before?" These prepared starters can help you feel more prepared and less stressed about making the first move.

Finding the right environment for networking can also play a crucial role in your comfort level. Smaller, more intimate gatherings are often more suitable for introverts. These settings allow for deeper, one-on-one conversations without the overwhelming hustle and bustle of large crowds. Look for events like small business mixers, niche industry meetups, or even book clubs related to your field. One-on-one meetings over coffee can be another excellent option. These quieter, more personal settings allow you to engage in meaningful discussions without the pressure of a large audience. Suggesting a coffee chat with someone you've connected with online or met briefly at a larger event can be a great way to build a connection in a more comfortable setting.

Managing energy levels is vital for introverts, as social interactions can be draining. Taking breaks to recharge during events can help you maintain your energy and focus. If the event spans several hours, find a quiet spot to step away for a few minutes. Use this time to gather your thoughts, take deep breaths, or simply enjoy a moment of solitude. Scheduling downtime post-event is equally important. After a networking event, give yourself time to unwind and recharge. Plan a quiet evening at home, engage in a relaxing activity, or spend time with close friends or family. This downtime helps you recover from the social exertion and prepares you for future networking opportunities.

Understanding Introvert Strengths

Introverts often excel in areas that are crucial for effective networking. Deep listening skills enable you to engage more fully with the person you're speaking to, picking up on important details and emotions. This ability to listen and understand can make your interactions more impactful, as people appreciate being heard and valued. Thoughtful and meaningful interactions are another strength. While extroverts may thrive on quick, surface-level conversations, you have the capacity to engage in deeper, more meaningful discussions. This depth can lead to stronger, more authentic connections, which are often the foundation of lasting professional relationships.

Preparing for Networking Events

Preparation is key to feeling more comfortable and confident at networking events. Start by setting specific goals for the event. Having clear objectives, such as meeting three new people or learning about the latest industry trends, gives you a sense of purpose and helps you stay focused. Practicing conversation starters in advance can also ease anxiety. Think of a few opening lines or questions that are easy to remember and natural to use. For example, you might start with, "What brought you to this event?" or "Have you attended this conference before?" These prepared starters can make initiating conversations less daunting and more manageable.

Finding the Right Environment

Choosing the right setting for networking can significantly impact your comfort and effectiveness. Smaller, more intimate gatherings are often better suited for introverts. These settings allow for deeper, one-on-one conversations without the overwhelming noise and activity of large crowds. Look for events like small business mixers, niche industry meetups, or even book clubs related to your field. One-on-one meetings over coffee can be another excellent option. These quieter, more personal settings enable you to engage in meaningful discussions without the pressure of a large audience. Suggesting a coffee chat with someone you've connected with online or met briefly at a larger event can be a great way to build a connection in a more comfortable environment.

Managing Energy Levels

Managing your energy levels is crucial for introverts, as social interactions can be draining. Taking breaks to recharge during events can help you maintain your energy and focus. If the event spans several hours, find a quiet spot to step away for a few minutes. Use this time to gather your thoughts, take deep breaths, or simply enjoy a moment of solitude. Scheduling downtime post-event is equally important. After a networking event, give yourself time to unwind and recharge. Plan a quiet evening at home, engage in a relaxing activity, or spend time with close friends or family. This downtime helps you recover from the social exertion and prepares you for future networking opportunities.

6.6 Maintaining Long-Term Professional Relationships

Imagine you've just made a fantastic connection at a networking event. The conversation flowed seamlessly, and you exchanged contact information with promises to keep in touch. But what happens next? For many, this is where the momentum stalls. Yet, nurturing professional relationships over time is crucial. Building trust and credibility takes consistent effort. It's not just about making a good first impression; it's about showing up repeatedly. When you maintain contact, you demonstrate reliability and commitment, which are cornerstones of trust. Over time, these qualities solidify your reputation, making others more likely to seek you out for advice, opportunities, or collaborations.

Long-term relationships create opportunities for collaboration. As you get to know your contacts better, you'll discover areas where your skills and interests align. These shared interests can lead to joint projects, partnerships, or even new business ventures. For instance, a casual acquaintance could become a valuable collaborator on a project that benefits both of you. These collaborations often blossom into deeper professional relationships, offering both parties the chance to learn, grow, and achieve more than they could alone.

Regular check-ins are vital for staying in touch and keeping relationships fresh. Scheduling periodic catch-up calls or meetings can help maintain the connection. These don't have to be lengthy or formal—sometimes, a quick coffee or a brief phone call can suffice. The key is consistency. Showing that you remember and value the relationship goes a long way. Sending occasional emails to share updates is another effective strategy. Whether it's a professional milestone, a new project, or even a relevant article, these updates keep the lines of communication open and demonstrate that you're thinking about the other person.

Offering value to your network is essential. Sharing relevant resources and articles can be incredibly beneficial. When you come across information that could help a contact, don't hesitate to pass it along. This shows that you're invested in their success and willing to support them. Making introductions and referrals is another powerful way to offer value. If you know someone who could benefit from meeting a contact, facilitate the introduction. This not only helps both parties but also positions you as a valuable connector within your network. Your willingness to give without expecting immediate returns builds goodwill and strengthens your professional relationships.

Celebrating milestones together can further solidify your relationships. Congratulating contacts on their achievements shows that you care about their success. Whether it's a new job, a promotion, or a personal accomplishment, taking the time to acknowledge these milestones can deepen your connection. A simple congratulatory email, a card, or even a small gift can make a significant impact. Inviting them to join in your own celebrations is equally important. Whether it's a professional achievement or a personal milestone, sharing these moments fosters a sense of mutual support and camaraderie. Celebrations provide opportunities to reconnect and reinforce the bond you share.

Maintaining long-term professional relationships requires ongoing effort and genuine interest in others. By building trust and credibility, creating opportunities for collaboration, staying in touch regularly, offering value, and celebrating milestones together, you can nurture strong, enduring connections. These relationships not only enrich your professional life but also open doors to new opportunities and collaborations. As we move into the next chapter, we'll explore how to build genuine connections that go beyond surface-level interactions, enhancing both your professional and personal life.

Chapter 7: Building Genuine Connections

Picture yourself at a family reunion, surrounded by relatives you haven't seen in years. Conversations buzz around you, but you feel a sense of distance. You want to connect with these people, to bridge the gap that time and space have created. The key to making these connections lies in empathy, a powerful tool that allows you to truly understand and resonate with others on a deeper level.

7.1 The Importance of Empathy in Communication

Empathy is the ability to understand and share the feelings of another person. It goes beyond mere sympathy, which is simply feeling pity or sorrow for someone else's misfortune. Sympathy often maintains a distance between you and the other person, whereas empathy bridges that gap, allowing you to experience their emotions as if they were your own. This fundamental difference makes empathy a far more effective tool for building genuine connections. Emotional empathy involves recognizing and sharing another person's emotional state, such as feeling their joy or sorrow. Cognitive empathy, on the other hand, is the ability to understand someone else's perspective and thoughts, even if you don't necessarily agree with them. Both forms of empathy are crucial for meaningful communication.

The benefits of empathetic communication are manifold. By enhancing mutual understanding and trust, empathy fosters stronger relationships. When you demonstrate empathy, you show that you value the other person's feelings and perspectives, which builds a foundation of trust. This trust, in turn, reduces conflicts and misunderstandings. When people feel understood and respected, they are more likely to communicate openly and honestly, leading to more productive and harmonious interactions. Empathy also encourages diverse perspectives and innovative solutions by creating an environment where everyone feels heard and valued. This inclusivity can lead to better decision-making and problem-solving, as it encourages input from all voices.

Developing empathy is a skill that can be cultivated with practice and intention. One practical step is perspective-taking, which involves putting yourself in someone else's shoes. This exercise helps you understand their experiences and emotions from their viewpoint. For instance, if a colleague is stressed about a project deadline, try to imagine the pressures they are facing and how it impacts their well-being. Engaging in active listening without judgment is another crucial practice. This means fully focusing on the speaker, acknowledging their feelings, and resisting the urge to interrupt or offer immediate solutions. Instead, validate their emotions by saying things like, "I can see why you feel that way" or "That sounds really challenging."

Empathy in action can be seen in various real-life scenarios. For example, consoling a friend during tough times requires genuine empathy. Instead of offering platitudes like "It'll be okay," take the time to listen to their concerns and feelings. Acknowledge their pain and offer your support by saying, "I'm here for you, and I understand how hard this must be." This approach not only provides comfort but also strengthens your bond with the friend. Similarly, supporting a colleague through a challenging project involves understanding their struggles and offering assistance without judgment. Instead of criticizing their efforts, offer constructive feedback and help them find solutions. Statements like "Let's work on this together" or "How can I assist you?" show that you are invested in their success and well-being.

Interactive Exercise: Practicing Empathy

1. **Identify a recent interaction where you could have been more empathetic.**
2. **Reflect on the other person's feelings and perspective in that situation.**
3. **Write down how you could have responded empathetically.**
4. **Commit to practicing this empathetic approach in your next interaction.**

Empathy is not just about understanding others; it's about creating connections that are genuine and meaningful. By practicing perspective-taking and active listening, you can develop your empathetic skills and build stronger, more trusting relationships. Whether you're consoling a friend, supporting a colleague, or simply engaging in everyday conversations, empathy is the key to unlocking deeper connections.

7.2 Techniques for Deep Listening

Imagine sitting across from someone who truly listens to every word you say, fully engaging with your story without a hint of distraction. This is deep listening, a practice that goes beyond active listening by immersing you completely in the speaker's world. Deep listening means engaging with the speaker on a profound level, focusing entirely on understanding their perspective rather than merely preparing your response. This form of listening requires you to be present, attentive, and genuinely invested in the conversation.

Being fully present during conversations is crucial for deep listening. The first step is eliminating distractions that can pull your attention away. Turn off phone notifications, close irrelevant tabs on your computer, and find a quiet space where you can focus without interruptions. Your undivided attention shows the speaker that you value their words and are fully engaged in the interaction. Beyond just hearing the words, pay close attention to nonverbal cues such as facial expressions, body language, and tone of voice. These elements often convey more than the words themselves and can provide valuable insights into the speaker's true feelings.

Reflective responses are a powerful tool in deep listening. They involve paraphrasing and summarizing the key points the speaker has made to ensure you truly understand their message. For instance, if a colleague shares frustrations about a project, you might respond with, "It sounds like you're feeling overwhelmed by the tight deadlines and lack of support." This technique not only validates the speaker's feelings but also clarifies any potential misunderstandings. Asking clarifying questions is another essential aspect of reflective responses. Questions like "Can you elaborate on that?" or "What do you mean by that?" encourage the speaker to provide more details and deepen the conversation.

Common barriers to deep listening include internal biases, preconceptions, and emotional reactions. We all have biases and preconceptions that can color our understanding of what others are saying. Recognizing and addressing these biases is crucial for truly hearing the speaker's message. For example, if you have a preconceived notion that a colleague is always negative, you might dismiss their valid concerns without really listening. Being aware of these biases allows you to set them aside and approach the conversation with an open mind. Managing emotional reactions is another challenge. It's natural to feel defensive or emotional, especially during difficult conversations. However, it's important to stay calm and composed, focusing on the speaker's words rather than your emotional response.

7.3 Building Trust Through Consistency

Consistency is the bedrock of trust in any relationship. When your actions align with your words, you create a predictable and reliable environment. This predictability fosters reliability, as others know they can count on you to follow through on your commitments. Transparency in your actions and decisions further enhances this trust. Being open about your intentions and sharing relevant information builds a foundation of honesty.

Maintaining consistent communication is essential for building and sustaining trust. Regular check-ins and updates with your contacts keep the lines of communication open. Whether it's a weekly team meeting or a monthly catch-up call with a friend, these interactions show that you care and are invested in the relationship. Keeping promises and following through on commitments is another crucial aspect. If you say you'll handle a task or attend an event, make sure you do. This reliability demonstrates that you are dependable and trustworthy.

Demonstrating reliability also involves meeting deadlines and honoring agreements. In a professional setting, delivering work on time and respecting project timelines shows that you take your responsibilities seriously. Being punctual and dependable in personal interactions, such as arriving on time for meetings or fulfilling social obligations, reinforces this trust. Consistency in these small actions builds your reputation as someone who can be relied upon.

Long-term consistency in behavior is vital for establishing a solid reputation for trustworthiness. Over time, maintaining consistent actions and communication patterns helps others predict how you will react in various situations. This predictability is comforting and fosters a sense of security in your relationships. Building a reputation for trustworthiness doesn't happen overnight; it requires sustained effort and dedication. By consistently demonstrating reliability, transparency, and dependability, you solidify the trust others place in you, creating stronger and more resilient connections.

7.4 Sharing Personal Stories to Connect

Sharing personal stories can be a powerful way to build connections. When you open up about your experiences, you create emotional resonance and relatability. People are naturally drawn to stories because they evoke emotions and make interactions more memorable. Sharing a story about a challenge you overcame or a lesson you learned invites others to see you as a real, relatable person. This vulnerability fosters a deeper connection and encourages others to open up as well.

Choosing the right stories to share is crucial. Your stories should be relevant to the conversation and your audience. If you're at a professional networking event, sharing a story about a career milestone or a work-related challenge can be more impactful than talking about a personal hobby. Additionally, stories that highlight vulnerability and growth are particularly effective. Sharing moments where you faced adversity and emerged stronger not only humanizes you but also inspires and motivates others.

Effective storytelling involves using vivid details to paint a picture and structuring your story with a clear beginning, middle, and end. For instance, if you're sharing a story about a challenging project, start by setting the scene and describing the initial problem. Then, explain the steps you took to address the issue and the obstacles you faced along the way. Finally, conclude with the outcome and the lessons you learned. This structure ensures that your story is engaging and easy to follow.

Encouraging others to share their stories is equally important for building connections. Asking open-ended questions about their experiences invites them to open up and share. Questions like "What inspired you to pursue this career?" or "Can you tell me about a time when you faced a significant challenge?" encourage detailed and meaningful responses. Creating a safe and supportive environment for sharing is also crucial. Show genuine interest in their stories, listen actively, and validate their experiences. This mutual exchange of stories fosters understanding and strengthens the bond between you.

7.5 Finding Common Ground in Conversations

Identifying commonalities with others is a key strategy for building connections. Common ground facilitates easier and more engaging conversations, as it provides a foundation for mutual understanding. When you find shared interests or experiences, you create a sense of camaraderie that makes interactions more enjoyable. This commonality also builds a foundation for deeper relationships, as it establishes a connection based on shared values or goals.

Finding shared interests involves asking about hobbies, interests, and experiences. Simple questions like "What do you enjoy doing in your free time?" or "Have you traveled anywhere interesting recently?" can uncover commonalities that spark engaging conversations. Listening for clues in the conversation is also important. Pay attention to what the other person mentions and look for opportunities to relate. If they talk about their love for hiking, and you enjoy outdoor activities too, you have an instant topic to explore together.

Connecting even when common ground is limited requires finding universal themes like values or goals. For instance, if you and the other person have different hobbies, you can still connect over shared values such as a commitment to personal growth or a passion for helping others. Being open and curious about the other person's perspective also helps bridge differences. Ask questions to understand their viewpoint and show genuine interest in their experiences. This openness fosters mutual respect and can reveal unexpected commonalities.

Specific examples of finding common ground can illustrate how to apply these strategies in real-life situations. At a networking event, discovering a shared love for travel can lead to interesting conversations about favorite destinations and travel experiences. Connecting over mutual professional challenges, such as navigating a difficult project or dealing with workplace changes, can also provide a strong foundation for building relationships. These shared experiences create a sense of understanding and empathy, making interactions more meaningful and enjoyable.

7.6 The Role of Vulnerability in Building Relationships

Vulnerability is an essential component of building genuine connections. When you show authenticity and openness, you invite others to see the real you, fostering trust and understanding. Sharing your true self, including your fears, hopes, and dreams, creates a deeper emotional bond with others. This authenticity strengthens relationships, as it demonstrates that you are willing to be honest and transparent.

The benefits of embracing vulnerability are significant. Encouraging reciprocal openness and trust is one of the primary advantages. When you are vulnerable, you signal to others that it is safe for them to be vulnerable too. This mutual openness deepens emotional intimacy in relationships, as both parties feel understood and accepted. Vulnerability also fosters a sense of belonging, as it creates a connection based on shared experiences and emotions.

Practicing vulnerability involves sharing personal experiences and feelings. For example, opening up about a recent challenge you faced or discussing a personal goal you are working towards can invite others to share their own stories. Admitting mistakes and asking for help are also powerful ways to show vulnerability. By acknowledging that you don't have all the answers and seeking support, you demonstrate humility and trust in others.

Overcoming the fear of vulnerability requires reframing it as a strength rather than a weakness. Recognize that being vulnerable is a sign of courage and authenticity. Building confidence through small acts of openness can help you become more comfortable with vulnerability.

Start by sharing something personal with a trusted friend or colleague, and gradually increase your level of openness as you become more confident. This practice not only enhances your ability to connect with others but also strengthens your self-awareness and emotional resilience.

7.3 Building Trust Through Consistency

Imagine you're working on a team project. One member consistently meets their deadlines and communicates openly about their progress. Over time, you begin to trust this person implicitly because their behavior is predictable and reliable. This is the essence of how consistency builds trust. When your actions align with your words, others know what to expect from you, creating a stable and dependable environment. Predictable behavior fosters reliability, which is the cornerstone of any trustworthy relationship. Transparency in your actions and decisions further reinforces this trust, as it eliminates ambiguity and promotes honesty.

Maintaining consistent communication is crucial for reinforcing this trust. Regular check-ins and updates with your contacts show that you value the relationship and are committed to maintaining it. Whether it's a quick email update, a phone call, or a face-to-face meeting, these touchpoints keep the lines of communication open and active. Keeping promises and following through on commitments is another key aspect. When you say you will do something, and then you do it, you demonstrate that you are reliable and trustworthy. These consistent actions build a strong foundation of trust over time.

Demonstrating reliability goes beyond just keeping promises. It involves meeting deadlines and honoring agreements consistently. In a professional setting, delivering work on time and respecting project timelines shows that you take your responsibilities seriously. It communicates that you are dependable and can be counted on to follow through. Being punctual and dependable in personal interactions also reinforces this trust. If you commit to meeting a friend for coffee or attending a family gathering, showing up on time and being fully present demonstrates your respect and reliability. These small actions collectively build a reputation for trustworthiness.

Long-term trust building is an ongoing process that requires sustained effort. Maintaining consistent behavior over time is crucial for establishing a solid reputation for trustworthiness. When others see that you consistently act in a reliable and predictable manner, they begin to trust your character and integrity. This consistency in behavior helps others predict how you will react in various situations, providing a sense of security and stability in the relationship. Building a reputation for trustworthiness doesn't happen overnight; it requires continuous effort and dedication. However, the rewards are well worth it, as you create stronger and more resilient connections that withstand the test of time.

To foster long-term trust, it's important to regularly assess your actions and ensure they align with your values and commitments. Reflect on your interactions and identify areas where you can improve your consistency. Seek feedback from trusted friends or colleagues to gain insights into how you are perceived and make necessary adjustments. By continuously striving for consistency in your actions and communication, you reinforce the trust others place in you and strengthen your relationships.

Consistency is not just about grand gestures or major commitments; it's about the small, everyday actions that collectively build trust. Whether it's sending a follow-up email after a meeting, showing up on time for a lunch date, or delivering on a promised project, these consistent behaviors demonstrate your reliability and integrity. Over time, these actions create a solid foundation of trust that enhances your personal and professional relationships.

Trust is a delicate and invaluable asset in any relationship. By embracing consistency in your behavior and communication, you create a predictable and reliable environment that fosters trust. This trust, once established, becomes the bedrock of strong, meaningful connections that enrich your life and the lives of those around you.

7.4 Sharing Personal Stories to Connect

Personal stories have a unique power to deepen connections. When you share your own experiences, you create emotional resonance and relatability. These stories often evoke emotions, making interactions more memorable and impactful. Think about a time when someone shared a heartfelt story with you. You likely felt a stronger bond with that person, as their vulnerability and openness drew you in. This emotional connection is the foundation of genuine relationships.

Choosing the right stories to share is crucial. Your stories should be relevant to the conversation and audience. If you're at a business meeting, sharing a story about a professional challenge you overcame can be more appropriate than recounting a personal anecdote about a family vacation. Relevance ensures that your story adds value to the interaction and keeps the audience engaged.

Additionally, stories that highlight vulnerability and growth are particularly powerful. Sharing moments where you faced adversity and emerged stronger not only humanizes you but also inspires and motivates others. These stories show that you are relatable and resilient, qualities that draw people closer.

Effective storytelling involves using vivid details to paint a picture. Instead of saying, "I had a tough time at work," describe the situation in detail. For example, "I remember the pressure mounting as the deadline approached. My desk was cluttered with papers, the phone kept ringing, and my heart raced with every passing minute." These details create a visual and emotional experience for the listener, making your story more engaging. Structuring your story with a clear beginning, middle, and end ensures that it is coherent and easy to follow. Start by setting the scene, then describe the challenge or conflict, and finally, share the resolution and the lessons learned. This structure keeps your audience hooked and provides a satisfying conclusion.

Encouraging others to share their stories is equally important for building connections. Asking open-ended questions about their experiences invites them to open up. Instead of asking, "Did you enjoy your trip?" try, "What was the most memorable part of your trip?" This type of question encourages detailed responses and deeper conversations. Creating a safe and supportive environment for sharing is also crucial. Show genuine interest in their stories, listen actively, and validate their experiences. Simple actions like nodding, maintaining eye contact, and offering verbal affirmations like "That sounds amazing" or "I can see why you felt that way" make the other person feel valued and understood. This mutual exchange of stories fosters understanding and strengthens the bond between you.

In a professional setting, sharing personal stories can break down barriers and build rapport. For instance, during a team meeting, sharing a story about a past project where you faced challenges and found innovative solutions can inspire your colleagues and build a sense of camaraderie. It shows that you are not just a professional but also a person who has faced and overcome obstacles. In social settings, personal stories can create lasting memories and deepen friendships. Sharing a funny or touching story at a gathering can make the evening more memorable and strengthen your connections with others.

Personal stories are not just about sharing your experiences; they are about creating connections that are genuine and meaningful. By choosing the right stories, using vivid details, and encouraging others to share, you can build stronger, more trusting relationships. Whether you're in a business meeting, at a social gathering, or just having a casual conversation, personal stories have the power to transform interactions and create lasting bonds.

7.5 Finding Common Ground in Conversations

Imagine you're at a social gathering, feeling a bit out of place. You spot someone you recognize but aren't quite sure how to approach. Identifying common ground can be the key to breaking the ice and building a meaningful connection. Commonalities facilitate easier and more engaging conversations, making both parties feel comfortable and understood. When you find shared interests, experiences, or values, you create a foundation for deeper relationships. These common points act as anchors, giving you both something to hold onto as you navigate the conversation.

One effective way to discover common interests is by asking about hobbies, interests, and experiences. Questions like, "What do you enjoy doing in your free time?" or "Have you traveled anywhere interesting lately?" can reveal shared passions. Listening closely for clues in the conversation is equally important. People often drop hints about their interests without explicitly stating them. For instance, if someone mentions they spent the weekend hiking, you can follow up with, "I love hiking too! What's your favorite trail?" This not only shows that you're paying attention but also opens the door to a more engaging dialogue.

Even when common ground seems limited, you can still find ways to connect. One approach is to focus on universal themes like values or goals. For example, if you both care about personal growth, you might discuss books or courses that have inspired you. Being open and curious about the other person's perspective also helps bridge differences. Ask questions to understand their viewpoint and show genuine interest in their experiences. This openness can reveal unexpected commonalities and foster mutual respect. You might find that, despite different hobbies or backgrounds, you share similar values or aspirations.

Specific examples can illustrate how to identify and leverage commonalities. During a networking event, you might discover a shared love for travel. This can lead to fascinating conversations about favorite destinations, travel tips, and memorable experiences. Connecting over mutual professional challenges is another powerful way to build rapport. If both of you are facing similar obstacles at work, discussing these challenges can create a sense of camaraderie and support. For instance, you might say, "I've been struggling with time management lately. How do you handle tight deadlines?" This not only provides valuable insights but also strengthens your connection.

Finding common ground is not just about identifying shared interests; it's about creating a sense of belonging and understanding. When you connect with someone on a deeper level, you build trust and empathy, making your interactions more meaningful. This approach is particularly effective in both personal and professional settings. Whether you're at a family gathering, a business meeting, or a casual social event, finding common ground can transform your interactions and create lasting bonds.

In a business context, identifying commonalities with colleagues can enhance teamwork and collaboration. Shared interests can lead to innovative ideas and solutions, as team members feel more comfortable sharing their thoughts and perspectives. For example, discovering that a colleague shares your passion for sustainable practices can lead to collaborative projects that benefit both the company and the environment. In social settings, finding common ground can make gatherings more enjoyable and inclusive. When everyone feels connected and understood, the atmosphere becomes more relaxed and engaging.

Ultimately, the ability to find common ground in conversations is a valuable skill that enhances your communication and relationship-building efforts. By asking the right questions, listening attentively, and being open to different perspectives, you can create connections that are both meaningful and enduring. These connections not only enrich your personal and professional life but also contribute to a more empathetic and understanding world.

7.6 The Role of Vulnerability in Building Relationships

Imagine standing before a group of colleagues, sharing a personal story of a professional failure. Your voice quivers slightly, but you push through, revealing your struggles and the lessons learned. This moment of vulnerability is powerful. Vulnerability is about showing authenticity and openness, allowing others to see your true self, complete with imperfections and fears. When you let down your guard and share your genuine experiences, you invite others to do the same. This act of openness can strengthen emotional bonds, creating a foundation of trust and mutual respect. Shared experiences, whether they are moments of triumph or times of hardship, weave a tapestry of connection that is far more resilient than one built on superficial interactions.

Embracing vulnerability brings significant benefits to your relationships. When you show your true self, you encourage others to reciprocate with their own stories and feelings. This reciprocal openness fosters a deeper level of trust, as both parties feel safe to be genuine without fear of judgment. Emotional intimacy deepens as you share your innermost thoughts and experiences, creating a bond that is both strong and resilient. Vulnerability also allows for richer, more meaningful interactions. When you share your struggles, you invite empathy and support, which can transform a simple relationship into a profound connection. This depth of understanding and trust is the cornerstone of lasting relationships, whether in personal or professional settings.

Practicing vulnerability requires intentional effort but is incredibly rewarding. Start by sharing personal experiences and feelings with those you trust. This could be as simple as discussing a recent challenge at work or a personal goal you are striving to achieve. Admitting mistakes and asking for help are also powerful ways to show vulnerability. For instance, if you are struggling with a project, reach out to a colleague and say, "I'm having trouble with this task. Can you help me?" This not only shows that you are human but also invites collaboration and support. These small acts of openness can gradually build your confidence in being vulnerable, making it easier to share more significant aspects of your life over time.

Overcoming the fear of vulnerability is a common challenge, but it is essential for building genuine connections. One effective strategy is to reframe vulnerability as a strength rather than a weakness. Recognize that being open and honest about your feelings and experiences takes courage and demonstrates integrity. This shift in perspective can make it easier to embrace vulnerability. Building confidence through small acts of openness is another practical approach. Start by sharing minor details about your life, such as a hobby or a recent experience, and gradually work your way up to more personal topics. Each act of openness will reinforce your confidence, making it easier to be vulnerable in more significant ways.

Vulnerability is not just about sharing your struggles; it's also about celebrating your achievements and allowing others to see your true self. When you share your successes and the hard work that led to them, you inspire others and build a sense of mutual respect. For instance, discussing a project you are proud of and the obstacles you overcame to complete it can motivate others to share their achievements and challenges. This mutual exchange of stories creates a supportive environment where everyone feels valued and understood.

In a professional setting, vulnerability can enhance teamwork and collaboration. When team members are open about their strengths and weaknesses, they can support each other more effectively. For example, if a colleague admits they are struggling with a particular aspect of a project, others can step in to offer assistance and share their expertise. This openness fosters a culture of collaboration and mutual support, leading to more successful outcomes. In personal relationships, vulnerability deepens emotional intimacy and trust. Sharing your fears, dreams, and experiences with loved ones creates a strong bond that can withstand the test of time.

As this chapter concludes, remember that empathy, listening, consistency, storytelling, common ground, and vulnerability are the building blocks of genuine connections. By embracing these practices, you can create deeper, more meaningful relationships that enrich your personal and professional life. Next, we will explore how to adapt these skills to different communication styles, ensuring you can connect with anyone, anywhere.

Chapter 8: Adapting to Different Communication Styles

Picture this: you're at a business meeting with a diverse group of people. As you present your ideas, some nod in agreement, while others seem disengaged. After the meeting, you realize that your message resonated with some but missed the mark with others. This scenario underscores the importance of adapting to different communication styles. Recognizing and adjusting to these styles can significantly enhance your interactions, whether with colleagues, clients, friends, or family.

Understanding Different Communication Styles

Communication styles can be broadly categorized into four types: assertive, passive, aggressive, and passive-aggressive. Each style has distinct characteristics that influence how messages are conveyed and received. Understanding these can help you navigate various interactions more effectively.

Assertive communication is characterized by a direct and honest expression of thoughts and feelings while respecting others' rights and needs. Assertive communicators use "I" statements, make eye contact, and maintain a straight posture. For example, they might say, "I feel concerned when deadlines are missed because it impacts our project timeline." This style fosters open dialogue and mutual respect, making it ideal for long-term relationships. However, it's sometimes misinterpreted as aggressive, especially in cultures where directness is less common.

Passive communication involves not expressing one's feelings or needs, often to avoid conflict. Passive communicators tend to defer to others, speaking softly, avoiding eye contact, and using phrases like, "I'm okay with whatever you decide." While this style can prevent immediate conflicts, it often leads to misunderstandings, resentment, and unmet needs. Over time, passive communication can erode self-esteem and strain relationships, as others may take advantage of the passivity.

Aggressive communication, on the other hand, is about expressing one's feelings and needs at the expense of others. Aggressive communicators often use a loud tone, interrupt others, and make demanding statements such as, "This is how it's going to be." They might also exhibit hostile body language, like crossing arms or rolling eyes. This style can quickly alienate others, leading to conflicts and damaged relationships. While it might result in immediate compliance, it generally undermines trust and respect.

Passive-aggressive communication is a blend of passive and aggressive styles. It involves appearing passive on the surface while subtly expressing anger or resentment. This style is marked by sarcasm, indirect communication, and behaviors like giving the silent treatment or spreading rumors. For instance, a passive-aggressive person might agree to a task but then deliberately perform it poorly. This style can create confusion and tension, as the true feelings are not openly addressed.

Assessing your own communication style is the first step towards improvement. Self-assessment quizzes can be a valuable tool for identifying your default style. Reflect on past interactions to see patterns in how you communicate. Do you often defer to others to avoid conflict, or do you find yourself raising your voice to get your point across? Understanding your tendencies can help you make conscious changes.

Recognizing others' communication styles involves observing both verbal and nonverbal cues. Pay attention to how people express themselves. Are they direct and clear, or do they avoid eye contact and defer decisions? Asking clarifying questions can also help. For instance, if someone seems reluctant to voice their opinions, you might ask, "How do you feel about this approach?" This not only shows that you value their input but also encourages them to communicate more openly.

Adapting to different communication styles requires flexibility and empathy. When interacting with assertive individuals, match their directness while maintaining respect. Use clear language and make eye contact. For passive communicators, create a safe space for them to express their thoughts. Ask open-ended questions and encourage them to share their views. With aggressive communicators, stay calm and composed. Acknowledge their points but assert your own needs without escalating the conflict. For passive-aggressive individuals, address the underlying issues directly but sensitively. Clarify any misunderstandings and encourage open communication.

Adjusting your tone and language is crucial for effective interaction. An assertive style benefits from a confident tone and precise language, while a passive style might require a softer approach. Using appropriate body language, like maintaining eye contact and open gestures, can further enhance your communication. By being aware of these nuances, you can navigate diverse interactions more effectively, fostering stronger and more respectful relationships.

Adapting to Introverts and Extroverts

Understanding the key traits of introverts and extroverts can dramatically improve your interactions with them. Introverts recharge their energy through solitude and tend to prefer deeper, more meaningful conversations. They often need time to reflect before responding and may feel drained by prolonged social interactions. In contrast, extroverts gain energy from social interactions and thrive in environments where they can engage with others. They enjoy a wide range of conversations, often favoring breadth over depth. Recognizing these fundamental differences can help you tailor your communication style to better connect with both introverts and extroverts.

When communicating with introverts, it's essential to allow them time for reflection and response. Introverts often need a moment to process information and formulate their thoughts before they speak. Rushing them or bombarding them with questions can lead to discomfort and withdrawal. Instead, give them space to think and respond at their own pace. Additionally, be mindful of overstimulation. Loud environments, rapid-fire questions, or constant interruptions can overwhelm introverts. Opt for quieter settings and more focused discussions to help them feel comfortable and engaged. Show that you value their input by actively listening and providing positive reinforcement.

On the other hand, engaging extroverts requires a different approach. Extroverts thrive on open and enthusiastic dialogue. They enjoy lively discussions and are often more expressive and animated in their communication. Encourage this by asking open-ended questions and showing genuine interest in their responses. Provide opportunities for social interaction, whether through group activities, collaborative projects, or networking events. Extroverts often find energy in these settings and are more likely to contribute actively. Be prepared for a more dynamic and fast-paced conversation, and don't be surprised if they interrupt occasionally. For extroverts, interruptions are often a sign of engagement and enthusiasm.

Balancing interactions between introverts and extroverts in group settings can be challenging but rewarding. Ensuring everyone's voice is heard requires a thoughtful approach. Start by creating an inclusive environment where both introverts and extroverts feel comfortable sharing their thoughts. For introverts, this might mean providing opportunities for written input or smaller group discussions before a larger meeting. For extroverts, it could involve structured activities that allow them to express themselves while ensuring they don't dominate the conversation. Facilitate the discussion by actively inviting input from all participants and acknowledging contributions from both introverts and extroverts.

Creating an inclusive environment also involves being mindful of the dynamics at play. Pay attention to nonverbal cues that indicate someone wants to speak but feels hesitant. Encourage quieter members to share their perspectives by directly inviting them into the conversation. For example, you might say, "I'd love to hear your thoughts on this, Alex," giving them a clear opening to contribute. Balance this with managing the enthusiasm of extroverts by setting ground rules for turn-taking and respectful listening. This ensures that everyone has a chance to participate and that the conversation remains balanced and productive.

By understanding the characteristics of introverts and extroverts and adapting your communication style accordingly, you can foster more meaningful and effective interactions. Whether in personal relationships, professional settings, or social gatherings, recognizing and respecting these differences can lead to richer and more satisfying exchanges.

Communicating Across Generations

Imagine you're working on a project with colleagues from different generations. Each person brings unique strengths and perspectives, but their communication preferences vary widely, impacting how effectively the group collaborates. Understanding these generational differences can significantly enhance your ability to connect and work together seamlessly.

Different generations have distinct communication preferences shaped by their experiences and technological comfort levels. Baby Boomers, born between the mid-1940s and mid-1960s, generally prefer direct, face-to-face communication. They value personal connections and tend to use formal methods like phone calls and in-person meetings. Their comfort with technology varies, but many appreciate a straightforward approach.

Generation X, those born from the mid-1960s to early 1980s, is adaptable and values concise and clear communication. They appreciate both email and face-to-face interactions, balancing traditional and modern methods. This generation values work-life balance and tends to favor straightforward, no-nonsense communication.

Millennials, born from the early 1980s to mid-1990s, are digitally adept and value open communication and recognition. They prefer interactive platforms like messaging apps and social media. This generation often seeks instant feedback and values transparency and inclusivity in communication.

Generation Z, born from the mid-1990s to early 2010s, are true digital natives. They are most comfortable with instant messaging, video conferencing, and collaboration tools. This generation values real-time feedback and thrives in diverse and inclusive environments. They prefer quick, informal communication and are adept at using technology to stay connected.

Adapting your communication approach to these preferences can make your interactions more effective. For older generations like Baby Boomers, using email and phone calls can be more effective. They appreciate the personal touch and directness of these methods. When working with Generation X, balance your approach by using both email and face-to-face meetings. Their preference for straightforward communication means you should be clear and concise.

For Millennials and Generation Z, leveraging social media and instant messaging is key. These generations appreciate quick, real-time communication and are comfortable with digital platforms. Use messaging apps for short, informal updates and social media for broader engagement. Video conferencing can also be effective, providing a more personal touch while maintaining the convenience of digital communication.

Bridging generational gaps involves finding common ground and building rapport across age groups. Focus on shared goals and values to create a sense of unity. For example, emphasize how each generation's unique strengths contribute to the team's overall success. Encouraging mutual respect and understanding is crucial. Acknowledge the different experiences and perspectives each generation brings to the table.

Specific scenarios can illustrate how to handle cross-generational communication effectively. Imagine collaborating on a multi-generational team project. Start by setting clear, shared goals that everyone can rally around. Use a mix of communication channels to ensure everyone stays informed and engaged. For instance, send detailed project updates via email for Baby Boomers and Generation X, while also using a messaging app for quick check-ins with Millennials and Generation Z.

Hosting a family gathering with diverse age groups presents another opportunity. Respect each generation's preferences by balancing activities and communication methods. Older family members might appreciate phone calls or face-to-face conversations, while younger members may prefer text messages or social media interactions. Create activities that everyone can enjoy, and encourage open conversations that allow each person to share their experiences and perspectives.

Understanding technological comfort levels is key. Older generations may need more support with digital tools, while younger generations might prefer using the latest apps and platforms. Be patient and offer assistance when needed, creating an inclusive environment where everyone feels comfortable participating.

Effective cross-generational communication requires empathy, flexibility, and a willingness to adapt. By tailoring your approach to each generation's preferences, you can enhance your interactions, build stronger relationships, and create a more cohesive and collaborative environment.

Tailoring Your Approach to Different Professional Roles

Understanding the communication needs and preferences of various professional roles can dramatically improve the effectiveness of your interactions. Each role within an organization has its own set of expectations and preferred ways of exchanging information. Managers, team members, and clients each have distinct ways of communicating that suit their responsibilities and functions. Recognizing these differences is crucial for building strong professional relationships and ensuring clear and efficient communication.

In hierarchical dynamics, communication can flow upward, downward, or laterally. Upward communication involves conveying information from subordinates to superiors, often focusing on reports, updates, and feedback. This type of communication requires clarity and conciseness to ensure that the message reaches the higher-ups without distortion. Downward communication, on the other hand, flows from managers to their team members, typically involving instructions, expectations, and performance feedback. It's essential that this communication is clear and motivational to keep team members aligned and engaged. Lateral communication occurs between peers or colleagues at the same organizational level. It often involves collaboration and information sharing, requiring a cooperative and respectful approach. Understanding these dynamics helps you tailor your communication style to suit the direction in which the information flows, ensuring that your message is received and understood correctly.

Role-specific jargon and terminology are also important considerations. Each professional role often has its own language, filled with specific terms and acronyms that may not be universally understood. For instance, a marketing manager might frequently use terms like "SEO" and "CTR," which could be confusing to someone outside the marketing department. Being mindful of this and adjusting your language based on your audience can prevent misunderstandings and enhance the clarity of your communication. When speaking with someone from a different department or role, take the time to explain or avoid jargon that might not be familiar to them. This consideration shows respect for their expertise and ensures that your message is accessible to everyone involved.

When communicating with managers and executives, being concise and focused is key. These individuals often have limited time and need to make quick, informed decisions. Present your points clearly and avoid unnecessary details that might clutter the core message. Supporting your arguments with data and evidence can significantly enhance your credibility and persuasiveness. Executives appreciate well-organized presentations and reports that highlight key insights and actionable recommendations. For example, if you're proposing a new project, outline the benefits, costs, and expected outcomes succinctly, and back up your claims with relevant statistics and case studies. This approach demonstrates your preparedness and respect for their time.

Engaging with team members requires a different approach, focusing on fostering open communication and collaboration. Encouraging idea-sharing and creating a supportive environment where everyone feels comfortable voicing their opinions can lead to more innovative and effective solutions. Regular team meetings and brainstorming sessions can provide platforms for collective input and feedback. Providing constructive feedback is also crucial. When offering criticism, focus on specific behaviors and outcomes rather than personal attributes. Use "I" statements to express your observations and suggest actionable improvements. For instance, instead of saying, "You're always late with your reports," you could say, "I've noticed that the reports are often submitted past the deadline, which impacts our project timeline. Let's discuss how we can ensure timely submissions."

Interacting with clients and customers demands a tailored approach that prioritizes understanding their needs and expectations. Building long-term relationships through personalized communication is vital. Start by actively listening to their concerns and asking questions to gain a deeper understanding of their requirements. Show empathy and acknowledge their perspectives to build trust. Tailor your communication style to match their preferences. Some clients may prefer detailed reports and formal meetings, while others might favor quick updates via email or instant messaging. Regular follow-ups and check-ins demonstrate your commitment to their satisfaction and help maintain a strong relationship. Personalizing your interactions, such as remembering their preferences or past interactions, can make clients feel valued and appreciated.

Understanding the unique communication needs and preferences of various professional roles can significantly enhance your interactions. Whether you're communicating upward, downward, or laterally, or engaging with managers, team members, or clients, tailoring your approach ensures that your message is clear, respectful, and effective. By recognizing and adapting to these differences, you can build stronger professional relationships and achieve better outcomes in your interactions.

Adapting to Cultural Communication Norms

Recognizing cultural differences is crucial for effective communication. Cultures vary widely in how they convey and interpret messages. High-context cultures, such as those in Japan and many Arab countries, rely heavily on context and non-verbal cues. In these settings, much of the communication is implicit, and the meaning is often inferred from the situation, the relationship, and the environment. On the other hand, low-context cultures, like those in the United States and Germany, depend on explicit verbal communication. Here, words are taken at face value, and clarity and directness are valued.

Understanding whether a culture favors direct or indirect communication styles can also make a significant difference. In direct communication cultures, people tend to be straightforward and clear in their expressions. They value honesty and openness and are not afraid to address issues head-on. In contrast, indirect communication cultures place a higher value on harmony and avoiding conflict. Here, messages are often conveyed in a more roundabout way, with a greater emphasis on non-verbal cues and implied meanings.

Researching cultural norms can help you navigate these differences. Start by reading cultural guides and resources. Books, articles, and online platforms offer a wealth of information about different cultural practices and communication styles. For example, understanding that in some cultures, maintaining eye contact is a sign of confidence, while in others, it may be seen as disrespectful, can prevent misunderstandings. Observing and asking questions when interacting with people from different cultures is also valuable. Pay attention to their body language, tone of voice, and reactions. When in doubt, asking polite questions about their preferences can show respect and willingness to adapt. For instance, you might say, "I want to make sure I'm communicating respectfully. Is there a preferred way you'd like me to address certain topics?"

Adapting your communication style based on cultural norms involves modifying both language and tone. In high-context cultures, it's important to be more subtle and read between the lines. Use phrases that are less direct and more suggestive. Instead of saying, "I disagree with this plan," you might say, "I wonder if there might be another way to approach this." Being mindful of non-verbal cues and gestures is equally important. In some cultures, certain gestures may have different meanings. For example, a thumbs-up gesture is positive in many Western cultures but can be offensive in parts of the Middle East. Observing the body language of those around you and mirroring their comfort levels can help you avoid unintentional missteps.

Consider the scenario of conducting business meetings with international clients. When meeting with clients from a high-context culture, start with small talk to build rapport before diving into business matters. Pay attention to their body language and tone. If they seem hesitant, they might be indirectly expressing concerns. Use open-ended questions to invite them to share their thoughts. In contrast, when dealing with clients from a low-context culture, be direct and clear. Present your points concisely and be prepared to answer questions directly. This approach shows respect for their time and preference for straightforward communication.

Navigating social interactions in multicultural environments also requires flexibility. Imagine attending a multicultural social event where you meet people from various cultural backgrounds. Start by observing the interactions around you. Notice how people greet each other, the level of formality in their conversations, and their body language. When engaging in conversation, use a neutral tone and avoid making assumptions about their communication preferences. If you're unsure, asking questions like, "How do you usually prefer to communicate in social settings?" can show your willingness to adapt and respect their cultural norms. This approach not only helps you communicate more effectively but also fosters mutual respect and understanding.

By recognizing and respecting cultural communication norms, you can enhance your interactions and build stronger, more meaningful relationships. Whether in business settings or social environments, adapting your communication style to align with cultural preferences demonstrates empathy and cultural awareness, paving the way for successful and respectful exchanges.

Navigating Digital and In-Person Communication

Navigating digital and in-person communication presents unique challenges and benefits. Digital communication offers speed and convenience, allowing you to connect with others instantly, regardless of geographic location. However, it lacks the nonverbal cues and body language that are integral to conveying emotion and intent. For instance, a simple text might be misinterpreted due to the absence of facial expressions and tone of voice. In contrast, in-person communication allows for richer interactions through eye contact, gestures, and physical presence, fostering deeper connections and understanding. Yet, it can be less convenient, requiring more time and effort to arrange.

Effective digital communication hinges on clarity and conciseness. When writing emails, be direct and to the point. Start with a clear subject line that reflects the content of your message. Use short paragraphs and bullet points to break up text, making it easier to read. For example, instead of a long, rambling email, write, "Attached is the report. Key points include: 1) Sales increased by 10%, 2) Customer satisfaction improved." This approach ensures your message is understood quickly and accurately.

Video calls offer a way to maintain personal connections in a digital world. They bridge the gap between digital and in-person communication by allowing you to see and hear each other. When using video calls, ensure your background is professional and free from distractions. Maintain eye contact by looking into the camera and use gestures to emphasize points, just as you would in a face-to-face meeting. This helps convey your message more effectively and keeps the interaction engaging.

Maintaining professionalism online is crucial for building and sustaining relationships. Set boundaries by managing your online presence. For instance, keep your professional and personal social media profiles separate. Be mindful of what you post and share. Always use appropriate language and tone in written communication, avoiding slang or overly casual expressions unless you know the recipient well. A professional tone shows respect and ensures your message is taken seriously.

Balancing digital and in-person interactions requires knowing when to switch from one to the other. Digital communication is excellent for quick updates and day-to-day coordination. However, for more complex discussions or when emotions are involved, transitioning to an in-person meeting or video call can be more effective. For example, if you're discussing a sensitive issue with a colleague, a face-to-face conversation allows for better understanding through nonverbal cues.

Maintaining personal connections in a digital world involves regular check-ins and thoughtful communication. Schedule periodic video calls or face-to-face meetings to strengthen relationships. Even in a digital-first environment, these personal interactions can make a significant difference. Send personalized messages to show you care. For instance, a quick "How are you doing?" text can go a long way in maintaining a connection. Remember birthdays, anniversaries, or significant events, and acknowledge them with a message or call.

Finding the right mix of digital and in-person communication is about balance and context. Use digital tools for efficiency but don't neglect the power of personal interaction. Each mode has its place, and understanding when to use each can enhance your communication effectiveness. Whether you're navigating professional relationships, personal connections, or social interactions, adapting your approach to suit the context can lead to more meaningful and successful exchanges.

Chapter 9: Practical Exercises for Communication Mastery

Imagine you're at a dinner party, and the host suddenly asks you to introduce yourself to the group. You feel your heart race and your mind goes blank. This scenario is not uncommon and highlights the importance of being prepared for various social interactions. Role-playing can be an incredibly effective method for practicing and perfecting communication skills. By simulating real-life situations, you can build confidence, receive immediate feedback, and adjust your approach in real-time. This chapter will guide you through various role-playing exercises designed to improve your ability to talk to anyone, anywhere.

Role-Playing Common Social Scenarios

Role-playing is more than just a practice exercise; it's a powerful tool for building real-world communication skills. It allows you to step into different scenarios, experience the dynamics of a conversation, and refine your approach based on immediate feedback. By simulating real-life situations, such as introducing yourself at a networking event or having a difficult conversation with a colleague, you can prepare for the unexpected and develop the confidence to handle any social interaction.

Common scenarios to practice include introducing yourself at a networking event. This exercise helps you refine your elevator pitch, practice making a positive first impression, and learn how to engage others in meaningful conversation. Another valuable scenario is having a difficult conversation with a colleague. This role-play can prepare you for addressing conflicts, delivering constructive feedback, and navigating emotionally charged discussions with tact and empathy.

To get the most out of role-playing, it's essential to follow some guidelines for effective sessions. Start by choosing a partner who can provide constructive feedback. This person should be someone you trust, who understands the purpose of the exercise and is willing to offer honest, helpful critiques. During the role-play, switch roles to gain different perspectives. For instance, take turns being the person initiating the conversation and the one responding. This dual perspective helps you understand the dynamics from both sides and improves your overall communication skills.

After the role-playing session, it's crucial to debrief and analyze the experience. Discuss what went well and what could be improved. Reflect on the emotional responses and reactions you experienced during the role-play. Did you feel nervous or confident? How did your partner's feedback align with your self-perception? This reflection helps you identify areas for improvement and reinforces the skills you've practiced.

Interactive Exercise: Setting Up a Role-Playing Session

Materials Needed:

- A trusted partner
- A quiet space
- A notebook for notes

Steps:

1. **Choose a Scenario:** Decide on the social interaction you want to practice, such as

introducing yourself at a networking event or having a difficult conversation with a colleague.
2. **Set the Scene:** Create a realistic environment that mimics the scenario. This could be a conference room for a business meeting or a casual setting for a social interaction.
3. **Role-Play:** Take turns playing different roles in the scenario. Focus on using the communication techniques you've learned, such as making eye contact, using open body language, and practicing active listening.
4. **Provide Feedback:** After each role-play, offer constructive feedback to your partner. Highlight what they did well and suggest areas for improvement.
5. **Reflect:** Use your notebook to jot down your thoughts and reflections on the role-play. Consider what you learned and how you can apply these insights to real-life situations.

Role-playing is a dynamic method to build and refine your communication skills. By simulating real-life scenarios, you can practice in a safe environment, receive immediate feedback, and make adjustments to improve your approach. Whether you're preparing for a networking event, a business meeting, or a personal conversation, these exercises will help you develop the confidence and competence to talk to anyone, anywhere.

Practicing Mindfulness in Conversations

Mindfulness in communication means being fully present and engaged during conversations. This involves more than just hearing words; it requires paying attention to the speaker's tone, body language, and emotions. Mindfulness helps you stay in the moment, reducing anxiety and improving focus. When you are mindful, you can respond more thoughtfully and authentically, making your interactions more meaningful. This practice also helps you manage distractions, ensuring that your attention remains on the person you are communicating with.

One way to practice mindfulness is through deep breathing techniques. Before entering a conversation, take a few moments to breathe deeply. Inhale slowly through your nose, hold the breath for a few seconds, and then exhale slowly through your mouth. Repeat this process several times to calm your mind and body. Deep breathing helps you center yourself, making it easier to stay focused and present during the conversation. During the interaction, if you feel your mind wandering, take a subtle deep breath to bring yourself back to the present moment.

Body scan meditations are another effective mindfulness exercise. Find a quiet place to sit or lie down and close your eyes. Starting from the top of your head, mentally scan down your body, paying attention to any sensations you feel. Move slowly down to your face, neck, shoulders, and so on, until you reach your toes. This practice increases awareness of your body and helps you release tension. By regularly practicing body scans, you can become more attuned to your physical and emotional states, enhancing your ability to stay present in conversations.

Integrating mindfulness into your everyday interactions can transform the way you communicate. Start by pausing to fully listen before responding. This means allowing the speaker to finish their thought without interrupting and taking a moment to process what they've said. This pause not only shows respect but also gives you time to formulate a thoughtful response. Another tip is to notice and let go of distractions. If you find your mind wandering to your to-do list or the noise outside, gently bring your focus back to the conversation. Acknowledging distractions without judgment and then refocusing helps you stay engaged.

Reflecting on your mindful communication experiences can provide valuable insights. Journaling about your interactions allows you to track your progress and identify patterns. After a conversation, take a few minutes to write down how you felt, what went well, and what could be improved. This reflection helps reinforce positive behaviors and address areas where you may struggle. For example, you might notice that you tend to interrupt when you're anxious. Recognizing this pattern allows you to work on being more patient and letting others speak without interruption.

Another way to reflect is by identifying areas for improvement. Pay attention to how you feel during and after conversations. Are there moments when you felt particularly present or distracted? Understanding these moments can help you refine your mindfulness practice. For instance, if you realize that certain topics make you anxious, you can prepare yourself with deep breathing exercises before discussing them. Regularly reflecting on your mindful interactions helps you become more aware of your communication habits and makes it easier to adjust and improve.

By practicing mindfulness in conversations, you can enhance your communication skills, reduce anxiety, and build stronger connections with others. Whether it's through deep breathing, body scan meditations, or simply staying present and engaged, these techniques can help you navigate social and professional interactions with greater ease and confidence.

Self-Assessment Tools for Communication Skills

Assessing your communication skills is a crucial step toward ongoing improvement. Self-assessment helps you identify your strengths and areas for development, allowing you to set specific goals for growth. Imagine trying to improve your physical fitness without knowing your current level of strength or endurance. Similarly, enhancing your communication abilities requires a clear understanding of where you stand. Self-assessment gives you this clarity, enabling you to focus your efforts where they are most needed and track your progress over time.

Creating a communication skills checklist can serve as a practical tool for this self-assessment. This checklist should include key aspects of effective communication, such as active listening and effective questioning. For active listening, consider whether you maintain eye contact, nod in agreement, and use verbal affirmations like "I see" or "That makes sense." These behaviors show that you are engaged and interested in what the other person is saying. Effective questioning is another critical area. Assess your ability to ask open-ended questions that encourage detailed responses and follow-up questions that show you are actively participating in the conversation. This checklist can help you monitor these behaviors and identify areas for improvement.

Feedback from others is invaluable in the self-assessment process. While self-reflection is important, external perspectives can provide insights you might overlook. Ask trusted friends or colleagues for their input on your communication skills. Be specific in your requests, asking questions like, "Do I make good eye contact during conversations?" or "How effective are my questions in keeping the conversation engaging?" Incorporate this feedback into your self-assessment to gain a more comprehensive understanding of your strengths and areas for growth. The combination of self-reflection and external feedback ensures a balanced and accurate assessment.

To make self-assessment a regular habit, set aside dedicated time each month for a self-review. During these sessions, revisit your communication skills checklist and evaluate your recent interactions. Reflect on what went well and identify areas for improvement. Tracking your progress over time can be incredibly motivating. Celebrate your improvements, no matter how small, as they contribute to your overall growth. This regular practice not only helps you stay focused on your goals but also reinforces positive behaviors and encourages continuous improvement.

Interactive Exercise: Monthly Self-Assessment Review

Materials Needed:

- A notebook or digital device for notes
- Your communication skills checklist

Steps:

1. **Review Recent Interactions:** Look back at your recent conversations and interactions. Reflect on how you communicated, using your checklist as a guide.
2. **Evaluate Performance:** Assess your performance in key areas such as active listening and effective

questioning. Note any patterns or recurring challenges.
3. **Gather Feedback:** If possible, ask for feedback from friends or colleagues who were part of these interactions. Incorporate their input into your self-assessment.
4. **Set Goals:** Based on your assessment, set specific goals for the next month. Focus on areas where you want to improve.
5. **Track Progress:** Keep a record of your progress toward these goals. Reflect on your achievements and areas for further improvement during your next review.

By regularly assessing your communication skills and setting targeted goals, you can ensure continuous growth and development. This proactive approach allows you to stay aware of your strengths and areas for improvement, making it easier to adapt and refine your communication strategies. Whether you're aiming to become a better listener, ask more effective questions, or simply engage more meaningfully in conversations, self-assessment is a powerful tool that can guide you on this path.

Real-World Networking Challenges

Networking can feel intimidating, but simulating networking events is an effective way to practice and build confidence. One way to do this is by organizing mock networking events with friends or colleagues. These simulated events can mimic real-life scenarios, providing a safe space to practice your skills. Invite a group of people, set up a casual environment, and take turns initiating conversations, introducing yourself, and engaging in small talk. This practice helps you get comfortable with the flow of networking interactions and allows you to experiment with different approaches without the pressure of a real event.

Role-playing different networking scenarios can also be incredibly beneficial. For instance, practice approaching a group of people who are already engaged in conversation. This situation often feels daunting, but with practice, you can learn to enter the conversation smoothly. Start by listening to the ongoing discussion, then find a natural moment to introduce yourself and contribute to the topic. Another scenario to practice is exiting conversations gracefully. Networking events often require you to move between multiple conversations. Develop a few polite exit strategies, such as, "It was great talking with you. I see someone I need to catch up with, but let's connect later."

Reflecting on your networking experiences is crucial for improvement. After each event or practice session, take some time to analyze what went well and what could be improved. Did you feel confident in your introductions, or did you stumble over your words? Were there moments when the conversation flowed naturally, or did you encounter awkward silences? Identifying these aspects helps you understand your strengths and areas for growth. Setting goals for future networking events based on this reflection is also essential. For example, if you struggled with small talk, set a goal to learn and practice three new conversation starters before your next event.

Networking can be especially challenging for introverts, but with tailored exercises, it becomes more manageable. Practicing small talk in low-pressure environments is a great starting point. Engage in casual conversations with coworkers, baristas, or neighbors. These interactions help you get comfortable with small talk without the intensity of a networking event. Another effective exercise is setting achievable goals for each networking event. Instead of aiming to meet everyone in the room, set a goal to have three meaningful conversations. This approach reduces the pressure and makes the event feel more manageable.

Overcoming networking hurdles involves proactive strategies. Approaching groups of people can be less intimidating if you prepare a few conversation openers in advance. For example, comment on the event or compliment someone's work if it's relevant. Remember to listen actively and look for opportunities to contribute to the discussion. When it comes to exiting conversations, having a few polite phrases ready can make it easier. For instance, you might say, "I've really enjoyed our chat. I'm going to mingle a bit more, but let's exchange contact information."

Simulating networking events and role-playing different scenarios provide a practical and safe way to build your networking skills. Reflecting on your experiences helps you identify areas for improvement and set specific goals. For introverts, practicing in low-pressure settings and setting achievable goals can significantly reduce anxiety. By addressing common networking challenges such as approaching groups and exiting conversations, you can develop the confidence and competence to network effectively in any environment.

Exercises for Building Empathy and Understanding

Empathy is the ability to understand and share the feelings of another. It's a crucial skill in both personal and professional relationships. One effective way to build empathy is through role-reversal exercises. Imagine you are in a heated argument with a colleague. Instead of standing your ground, take a moment to see the situation from their perspective. What might they be feeling? What pressures might they be under? By switching roles, you gain insight into their emotional state, which can help you respond more compassionately. This exercise not only enhances your empathy but also helps you understand the underlying issues better.

Active listening drills are another powerful way to build empathy. In these drills, focus entirely on the speaker. Pay attention to their words, tone, and body language. Resist the urge to interrupt or formulate your response while they are speaking. Instead, nod and use verbal affirmations to show you are engaged. After they finish, reflect back what you've heard using phrases like, "It sounds like you're feeling..." or "I hear that you're concerned about..." These drills help you practice being fully present and show the speaker that their feelings and thoughts are valid and important.

Integrating empathetic communication into your daily interactions can significantly improve your relationships. Start by using empathetic statements. When someone shares a problem or concern, respond with phrases like, "I can see how that would be challenging" or "It sounds like you're really stressed about this." These statements acknowledge the other person's feelings without judgment. Asking questions to understand others' feelings further deepens your connection. Instead of assuming you know how they feel, ask, "How does that make you feel?" or "What has been the hardest part for you?" This shows that you care about their emotional experience and are willing to listen.

Reflecting on your empathy-building experiences is essential for growth. Keeping a journal can be a valuable tool. After an interaction where you practiced empathy, write down what happened. How did you feel? How did the other person respond? What went well, and what could be improved? This reflection helps you identify your emotional responses and growth areas. You might notice patterns, such as feeling more connected when you use empathetic statements or recognizing that you interrupt less when you focus entirely on the speaker. These insights can guide you in becoming more empathetic over time.

Empathy is not limited to personal interactions. It plays a vital role in professional settings as well. Supporting a colleague through a stressful project, for example, requires empathy. Instead of just focusing on the task, take time to understand their pressures and concerns. Ask how you can help and offer support, whether it's by taking on some of their workload or simply being a sounding board for their frustrations. Being present for a friend during a difficult time also showcases empathy. Sometimes, just being there and listening without offering solutions is the best support you can provide. Your presence alone can be incredibly comforting.

In different contexts, empathy can manifest in various ways. In a business setting, showing empathy might involve understanding a client's concerns and addressing them with sensitivity. In sales, it means listening to a customer's needs and finding solutions that genuinely help them. In personal relationships, empathy fosters deeper connections and mutual understanding. By practicing empathy in various settings, you can improve your ability to connect with others on a profound level, making your interactions more meaningful and fulfilling.

Developing a Personal Communication Improvement Plan

Creating a personalized communication improvement plan is crucial for anyone aiming to enhance their ability to connect effectively with others. Tailoring a plan to your unique needs ensures you focus on the areas that will make the most significant impact. To start, set specific, measurable goals. This means identifying clear objectives you want to achieve, such as improving your public speaking skills or becoming a better listener. Measurable goals allow you to track your progress and adjust your strategies as needed. For example, instead of saying, "I want to be a better communicator," specify, "I want to improve my public speaking by practicing once a week and seeking feedback."

Identifying key areas for focus and development is the next step. Conduct a thorough self-assessment to pinpoint your strengths and weaknesses. This involves reflecting on past interactions and considering feedback from others. Are you good at initiating conversations but struggle with maintaining them? Do you find it challenging to understand nonverbal cues? Recognizing these areas helps you prioritize your efforts and allocate your time and resources effectively. Additionally, consider the contexts in which you want to improve, whether it's in professional settings, personal relationships, or social gatherings.

To develop your plan, start with a step-by-step guide. Begin by conducting a self-assessment to identify your strengths and weaknesses. Reflect on your past interactions, noting what went well and what could be improved. Seek feedback from trusted friends or colleagues to gain external perspectives. This comprehensive assessment provides a clear picture of your current communication skills. Next, set short-term and long-term communication goals. Short-term goals might include practicing active listening in daily conversations, while long-term goals could involve becoming a more confident public speaker or improving your ability to handle difficult conversations.

Implementing the plan requires dedication and consistency. Schedule regular practice sessions to work on your communication skills. This could involve practicing public speaking, engaging in role-playing exercises, or participating in networking events. Consistent practice helps reinforce new skills and build confidence. Additionally, seek feedback and make adjustments as needed. After each practice session or real-life interaction, ask for feedback from others. Use this feedback to refine your approach and make necessary improvements. Remember, communication is a dynamic skill that evolves with practice and reflection.

Tracking your progress and adjusting goals is essential for continuous improvement. Keep a communication journal to document your experiences, reflections, and progress. Note the techniques you practiced, the feedback you received, and any challenges you encountered. This journal serves as a valuable tool for self-reflection and helps you stay accountable to your goals. Regularly review and revise your plan based on your progress. If you achieve a short-term goal, set a new one to keep pushing yourself. If you encounter obstacles, adjust your strategies to overcome them. This iterative process ensures that your improvement plan remains relevant and effective.

By developing a personalized communication improvement plan, you can take control of your growth and make meaningful strides in your ability to connect with others. Setting specific, measurable goals, identifying key areas for focus, and following a step-by-step guide provides a structured approach to improvement. Implementing the plan with regular practice and feedback ensures that you stay on track and make continuous progress. Tracking your progress and adjusting goals as needed helps you stay motivated and accountable. This comprehensive approach to improving your communication skills will empower you to navigate any social or professional setting with confidence and ease.

Dear Reader,

Thank you for choosing *How to Talk to Anyone*! We hope you're finding the insights and strategies useful. As you're at the end through the book, we'd love to hear your thoughts!

Your feedback at this stage can help us understand how the content resonates with you. Whether you're finding certain sections particularly helpful, or you have suggestions for improvement, we'd love to hear from you!

Your input will help us ensure that *How to Talk to Anyone* meets your expectations and continues to provide value.

How to Leave Your Review: Please take a moment to share your thoughts by leaving a review on the platform (Amazon) or by clicking on the link below.

https://www.amazon.com/How-talk-anyone-ebook/dp/B0DHPSX68S/

Thank you for your time, and we look forward to hearing your feedback!

Best regards,

Debra Miller

Conclusion

The journey through this book was designed to empower you to have successful conversations in both business and personal environments. The purpose has always been to equip you with the skills and confidence to navigate any social setting, making each interaction an opportunity for connection and growth.

Throughout the chapters, we have delved into various aspects of communication, each contributing to the overall goal of mastering the art of conversation.

Building Confidence in Social Settings: We began by addressing the anxiety that often accompanies social interactions. By mastering first impressions, overcoming social anxiety, and employing strategies to start conversations, you can transform nervousness into confidence.

Mastering Nonverbal Communication: This chapter emphasized the importance of gestures, facial expressions, and eye contact. Understanding and using nonverbal cues effectively can significantly enhance your ability to connect with others.

Keeping Conversations Engaging: We explored techniques for crafting effective icebreakers, active listening, and asking open-ended questions. These skills ensure that your conversations remain lively and meaningful.

Navigating Difficult Conversations: Difficult conversations are inevitable, but with preparation, mindfulness, and conflict resolution strategies, you can handle them with confidence and tact.

Effective Networking Strategies: Networking is crucial for career and personal growth. By crafting a memorable elevator pitch, following up effectively, and leveraging social media, you can build a robust professional network.

Building Genuine Connections: Empathy, deep listening, and consistency are key to forming genuine connections. Sharing personal stories and finding common ground strengthens relationships.

Adapting to Different Communication Styles: Understanding and adapting to various communication styles, generational preferences, and cultural norms ensures that you can connect with anyone, anywhere.

Practical Exercises for Communication Mastery: Role-playing common scenarios, practicing mindfulness, and creating a personal communication improvement plan are essential for continuous growth.

Key Takeaways:

1. First impressions matter; your appearance, body language, and verbal introductions set the tone.
2. Nonverbal cues are powerful; use them to convey confidence and empathy.
3. Active listening and asking open-ended questions keep conversations engaging.
4. Mindfulness and preparation are critical for navigating difficult conversations.
5. Effective networking relies on a strong elevator pitch and timely follow-ups.

6. Building genuine connections requires empathy, deep listening, and consistency.
7. Adapting to different communication styles and cultural norms enhances your ability to connect.
8. Regular practice and continuous improvement are essential for mastering communication skills.

Reflecting on the journey of writing this book, I am reminded of my own experiences in real estate, banking, and finance. Each interaction, whether closing a deal or resolving a conflict, taught me the value of effective communication. My passion for helping others improve their communication abilities stems from these experiences. I believe that everyone has the potential to become a confident and effective communicator.

I encourage you to actively apply the techniques you have learned. Practice regularly and seek continuous improvement. Join support groups, attend workshops, or find a mentor to further enhance your skills. The more you engage with these practices, the more natural and effective your communication will become.

As you embrace the art of conversation, remember to do so with confidence, empathy, and authenticity. Effective communication can profoundly impact your personal and professional lives. It opens doors to new opportunities, strengthens relationships, and fosters mutual understanding.

You have the tools and knowledge to transform your interactions. Go forth with the confidence that you can talk to anyone, anywhere, and make each conversation a meaningful connection.

References

- *First Impressions Matter: The Primacy Effect* https://www.opentextbooks.org.hk/ditatopic/16473
- *Mindfulness Tips for Easing Social Anxiety* https://connect2affect.org/mindfulness-tips-for-easing-social-anxiety/
- *200 Engaging Icebreaker Questions* https://conversationstartersworld.com/icebreaker-questions/
- *Assertive Communication: What It Means and How to Use It* https://www.verywellmind.com/learn-assertive-communication-in-five-simple-steps-3144969
- *23 Essential Body Language Examples and Their Meanings* https://www.scienceofpeople.com/body-language-examples/
- *4.4 Nonverbal Communication and Culture* https://open.maricopa.edu/com110/chapter/4-4-nonverbal-communication-in-context/
- *The Psychology of Mirroring - Imagine Health* https://imaginehealth.ie/the-psychology-of-mirroring/
- *How to Overcome Eye Contact Anxiety - Verywell Mind* https://www.verywellmind.com/how-do-i-maintain-good-eye-contact-3024392
- *Icebreaker Questions: Why They Matter* https://www.parabol.co/blog/icebreaker-questions-why-they-matter/
- *7 Active Listening Techniques For Better Communication*

- https://www.verywellmind.com/what-is-active-listening-3024343
- *How do open-ended questions improve interpersonal ...* https://drwilliamlane.medium.com/how-do-open-ended-questions-improve-interpersonal-communication-7bdef30d0604
- *8 Classic storytelling techniques for engaging presentations* https://blog.sparkol.com/8-classic-storytelling-techniques-for-engaging-presentations
- *4 Things to Do Before a Tough Conversation* https://hbr.org/2019/01/4-things-to-do-before-a-tough-conversation
- *How to stay calm under pressure — Calm Blog* https://www.calm.com/blog/how-to-stay-calm-under-pressure
- *5 Strategies for Conflict Resolution in the Workplace* https://online.hbs.edu/blog/post/strategies-for-conflict-resolution-in-the-workplace
- *The Art Of Delivering Constructive Feedback* https://www.forbes.com/councils/forbesbusinesscouncil/2023/02/09/the-art-of-delivering-constructive-feedback/
- *23 Elevator Pitch Examples to Inspire Your Own [+ ...* https://blog.hubspot.com/sales/elevator-pitch-examples
- *Follow Up and Follow through For More Impactful Networking* https://psinc.io/articles/follow-up-and-follow-through-for-more-impactful-networking/
- *Top Five Social Media Platforms For Business Leaders* https://www.forbes.com/councils/forbescoachesc

ouncil/2021/03/09/top-five-social-media-platforms-for-business-leaders/
- *Networking for Introverts: 7 Tips for Making Better ...* https://www.indeed.com/career-advice/career-development/networking-for-introverts
- *The Role of Empathy in Communication* https://www.linkedin.com/pulse/role-empathy-communication-why-understanding-your-tyler-mehigh-mba
- *How to Engage in Deep Listening in the Workplace* https://pumble.com/blog/deep-listening/
- *Consistency Builds Trust & Confidence - Galen Emanuele* https://galenemanuele.com/blog/consistency-builds-trust#:~:text=One%20of%20the%20most%20effective,with%20your%20behavior%20is%20key.
- *The Power of Storytelling to Facilitate Human Connection ...* https://sites.bu.edu/impact/previous-issues/impact-summer-2022/the-power-of-storytelling/
- *Understanding Your Communication Style - UMatter* https://umatter.princeton.edu/respect/tools/communication-styles
- *How Introverts and Extroverts Can Talk to Each Other* https://experiencelife.lifetime.life/article/lost-in-translation/
- *Communication Styles in the Workplace: Gen Z, Boomer & ...* https://powell-software.com/resources/blog/communication-styles/

- *How to Adapt Your Communication Style with Clients* https://www.linkedin.com/advice/0/how-can-you-adapt-your-communication-style-when-tquee
- *Teaching Communication Skills Using Role-Play* https://www.ncbi.nlm.nih.gov/pmc/articles/PMC3155105/
- *Mindful listening: how to improve your communication* https://www.calm.com/blog/mindful-listening
- *How Good Are Your Communication Skills?* https://www.mindtools.com/a3y5cte/how-good-are-your-communication-skills
- *5 Networking Tips for Introverts (and Anyone Else)* https://hbr.org/2024/04/5-networking-tips-for-introverts-and-anyone-else

Printed in Great Britain
by Amazon